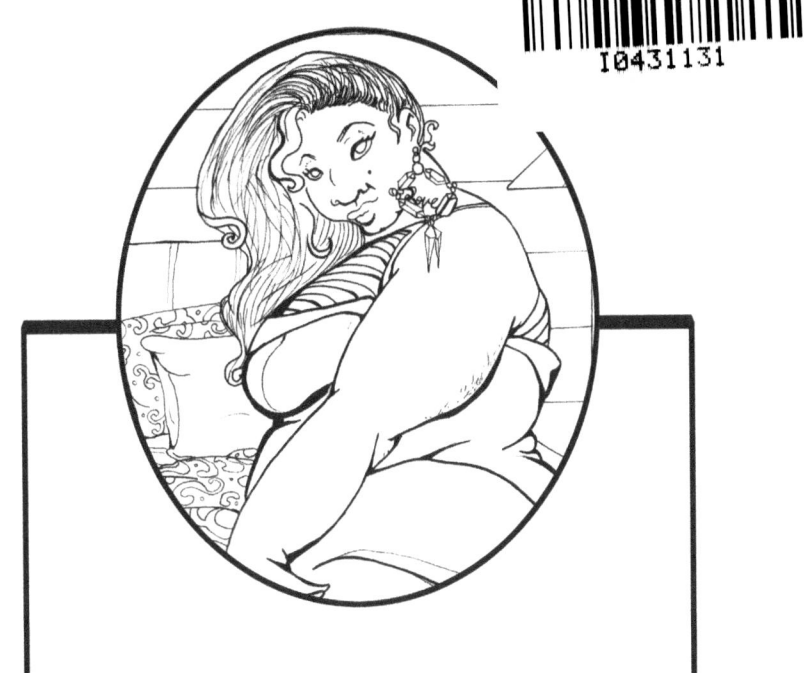

Beautiful Bodies

A Collection of Human Experience

Illustrated by
Alexis Reehill

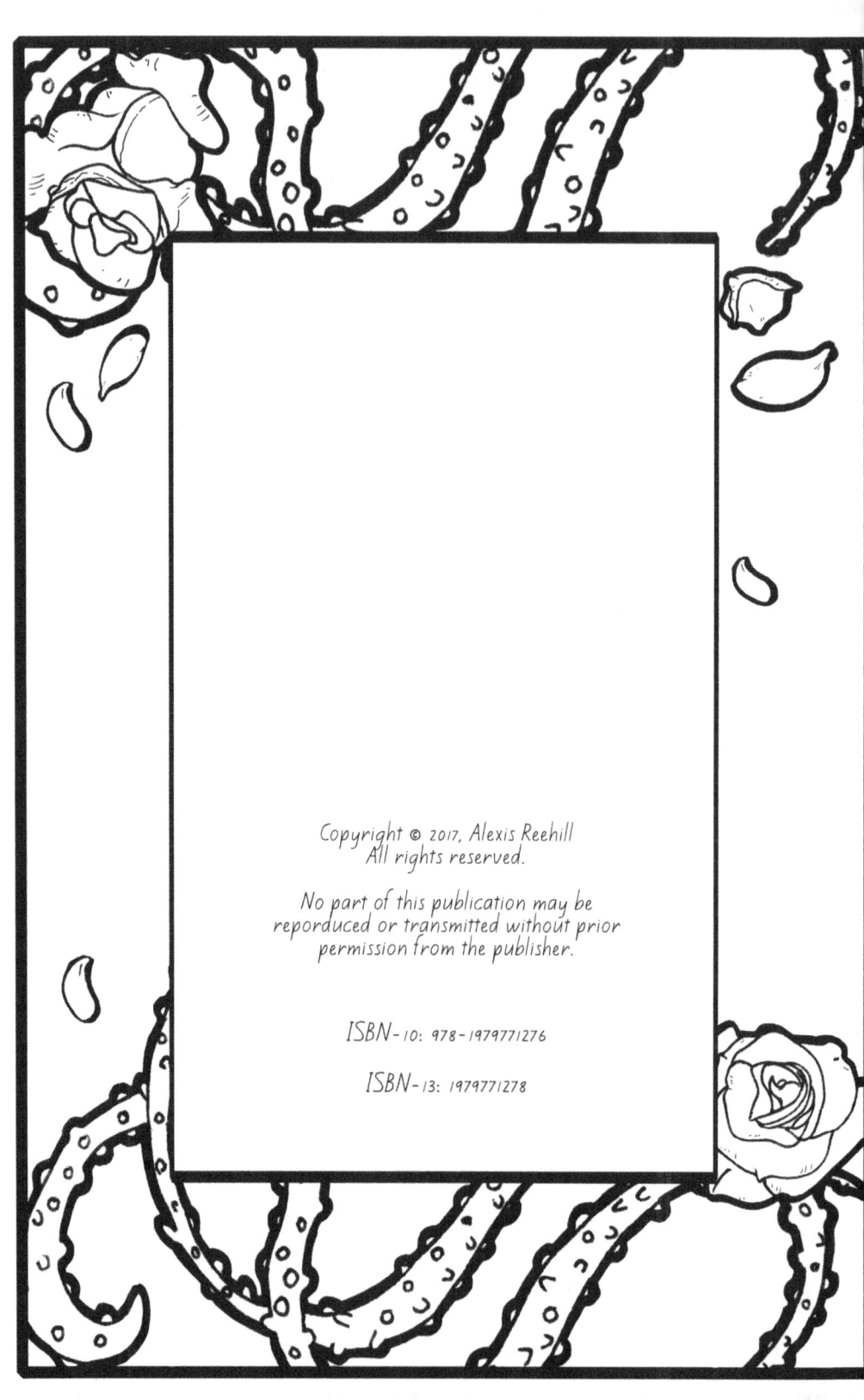

Copyright © 2017, Alexis Reehill
All rights reserved.

No part of this publication may be reporduced or transmitted without prior permission from the publisher.

ISBN-10: 978-1979771276

ISBN-13: 1979771278

For the ones left out, overlooked, and ignored:
I see you.

You have worth.

You are beautiful.

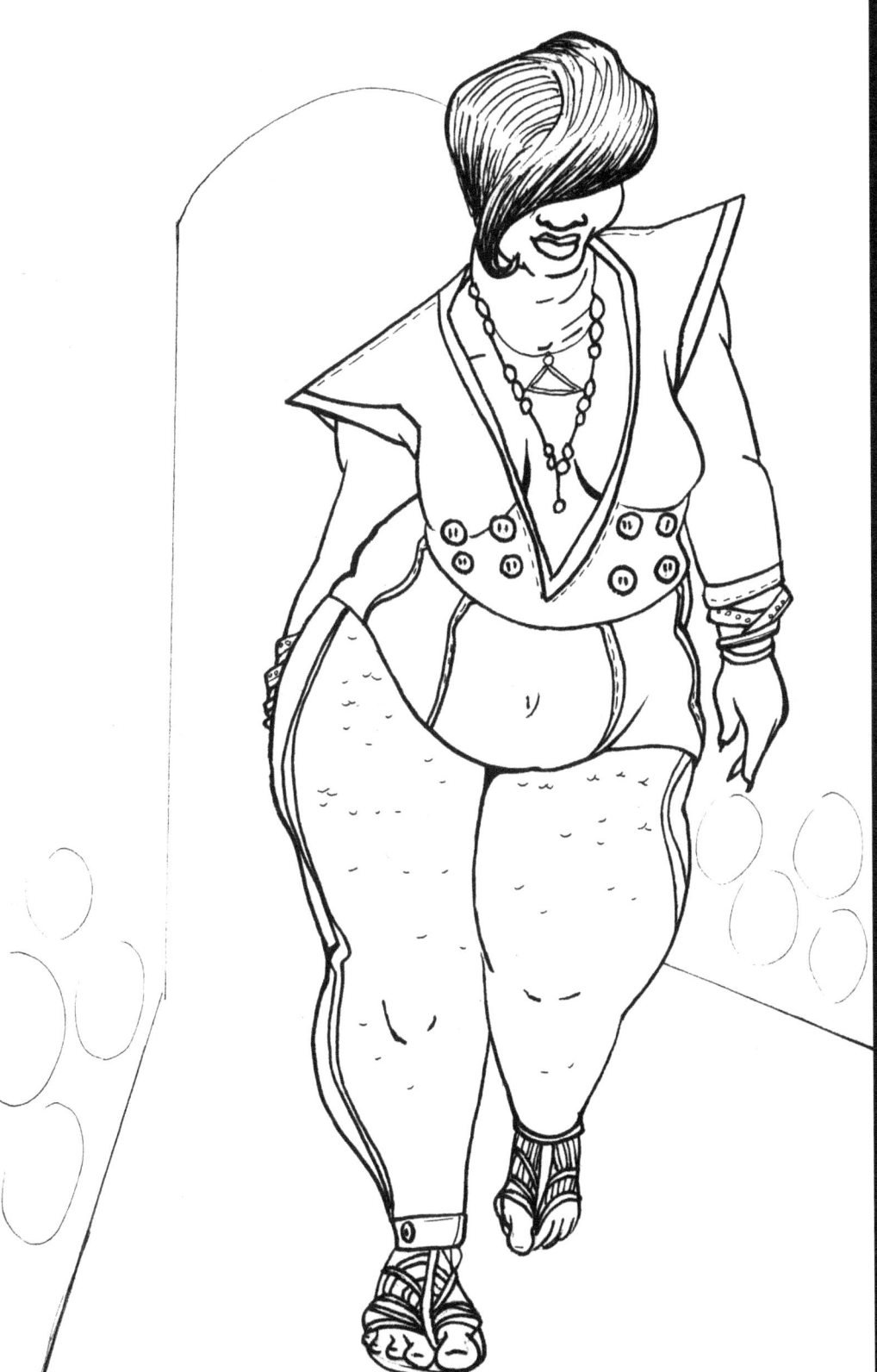

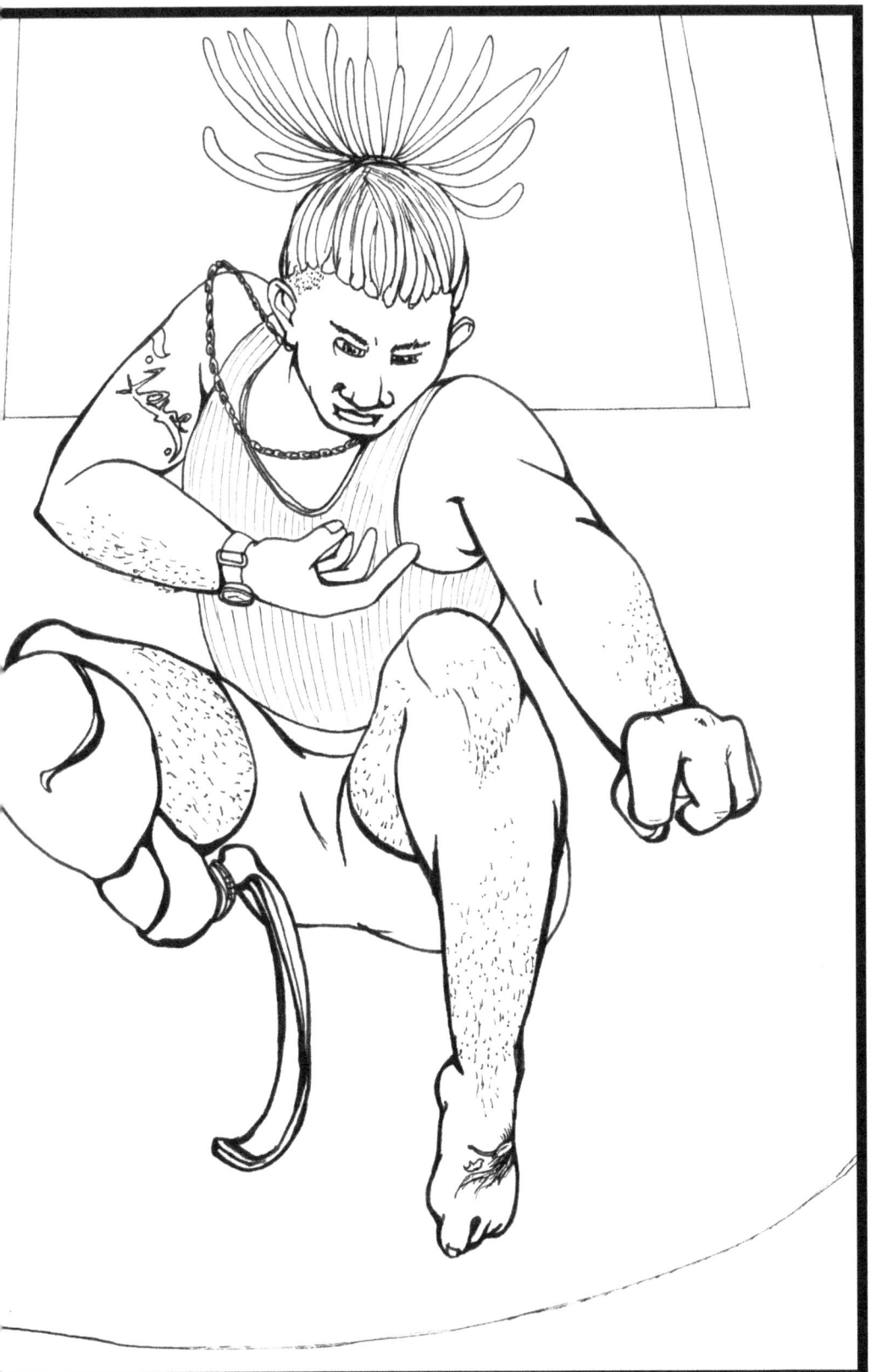

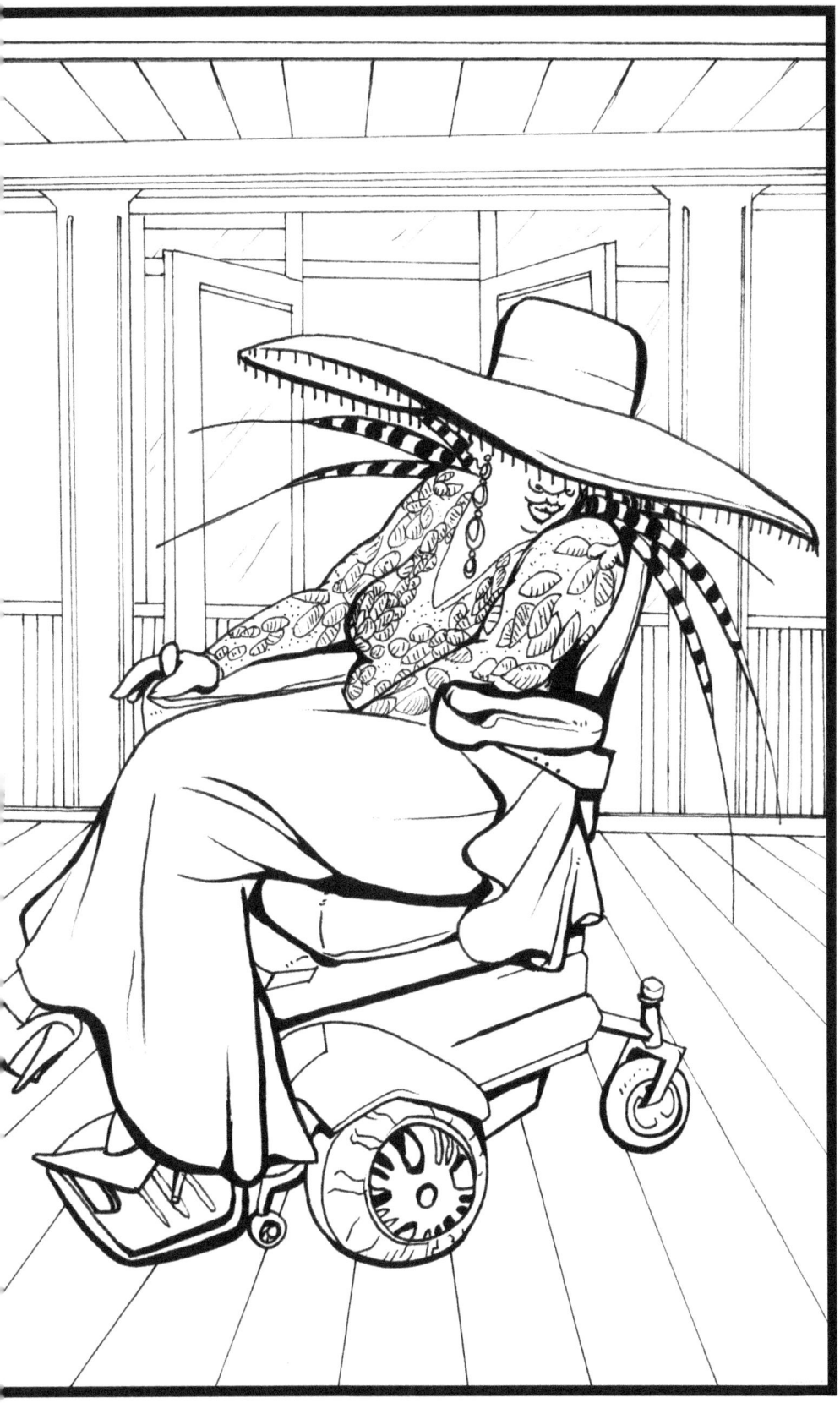

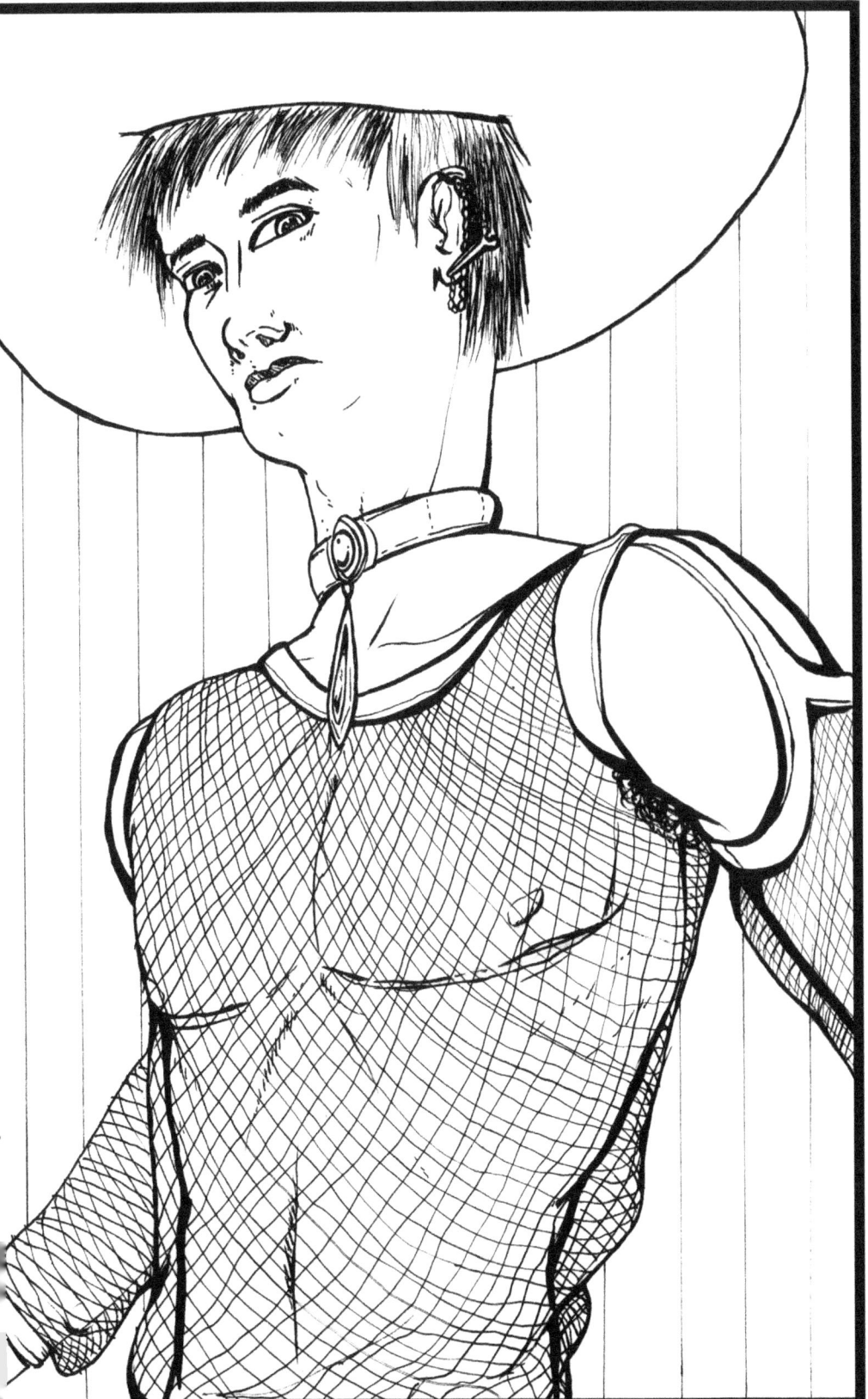

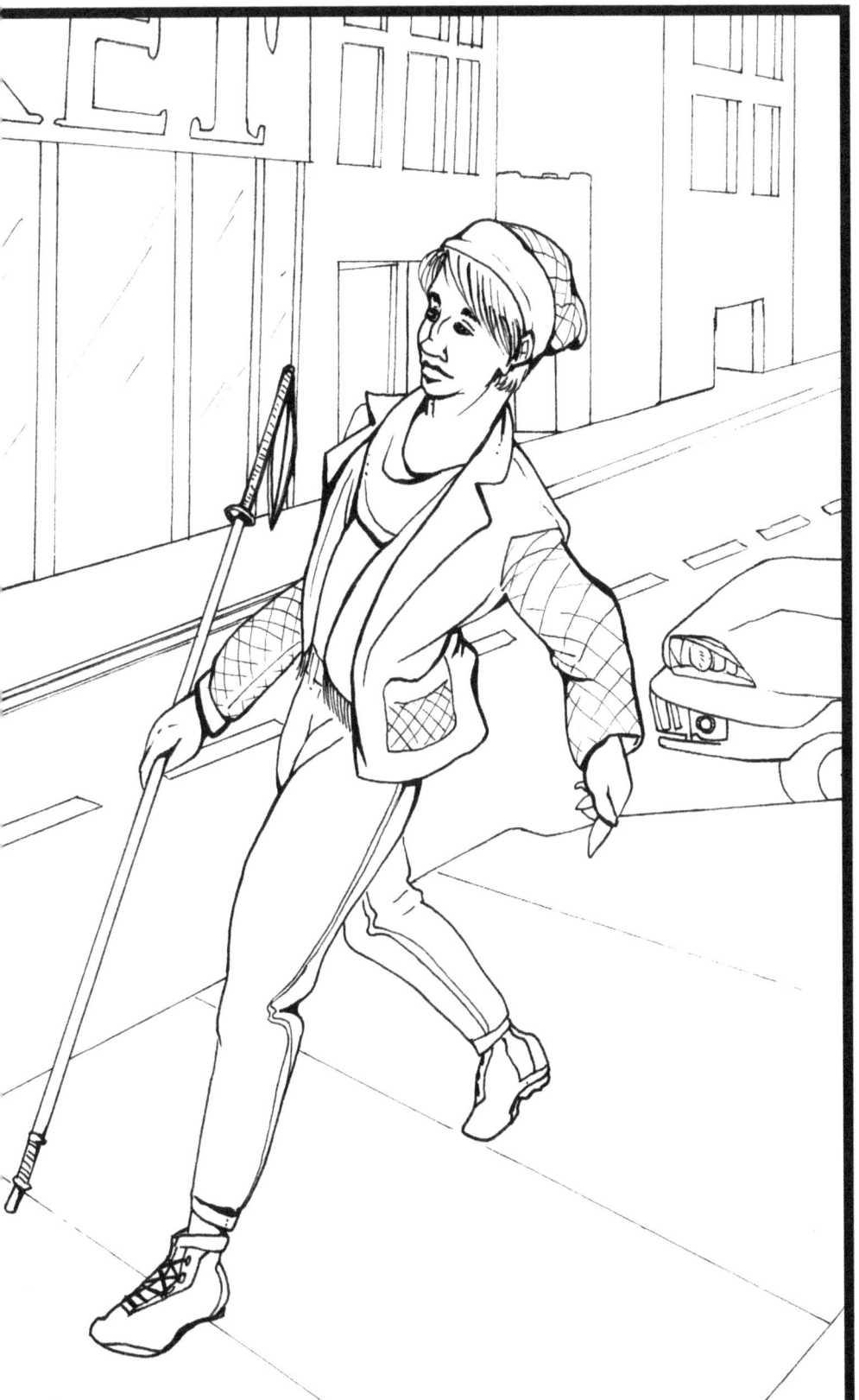

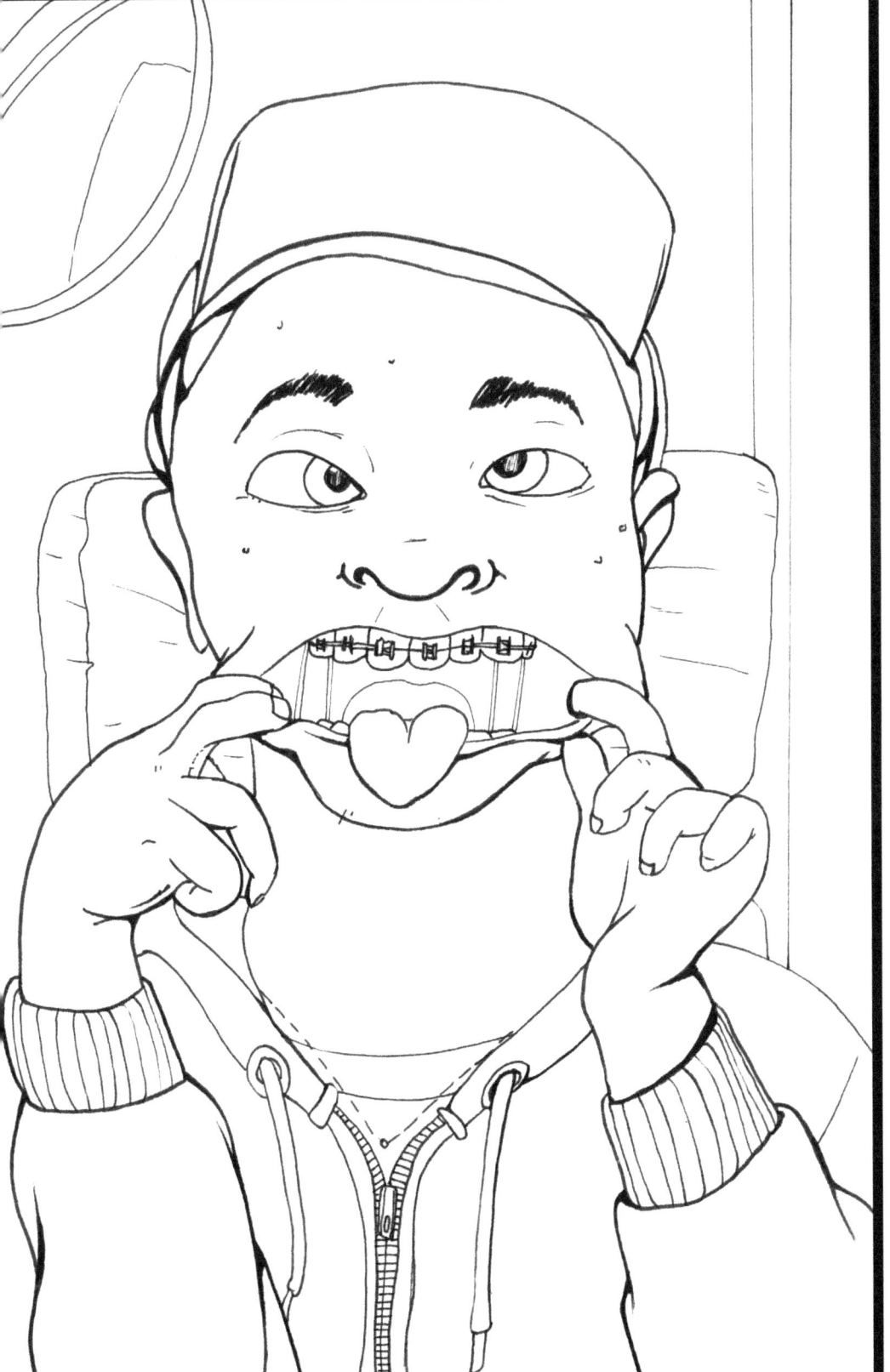

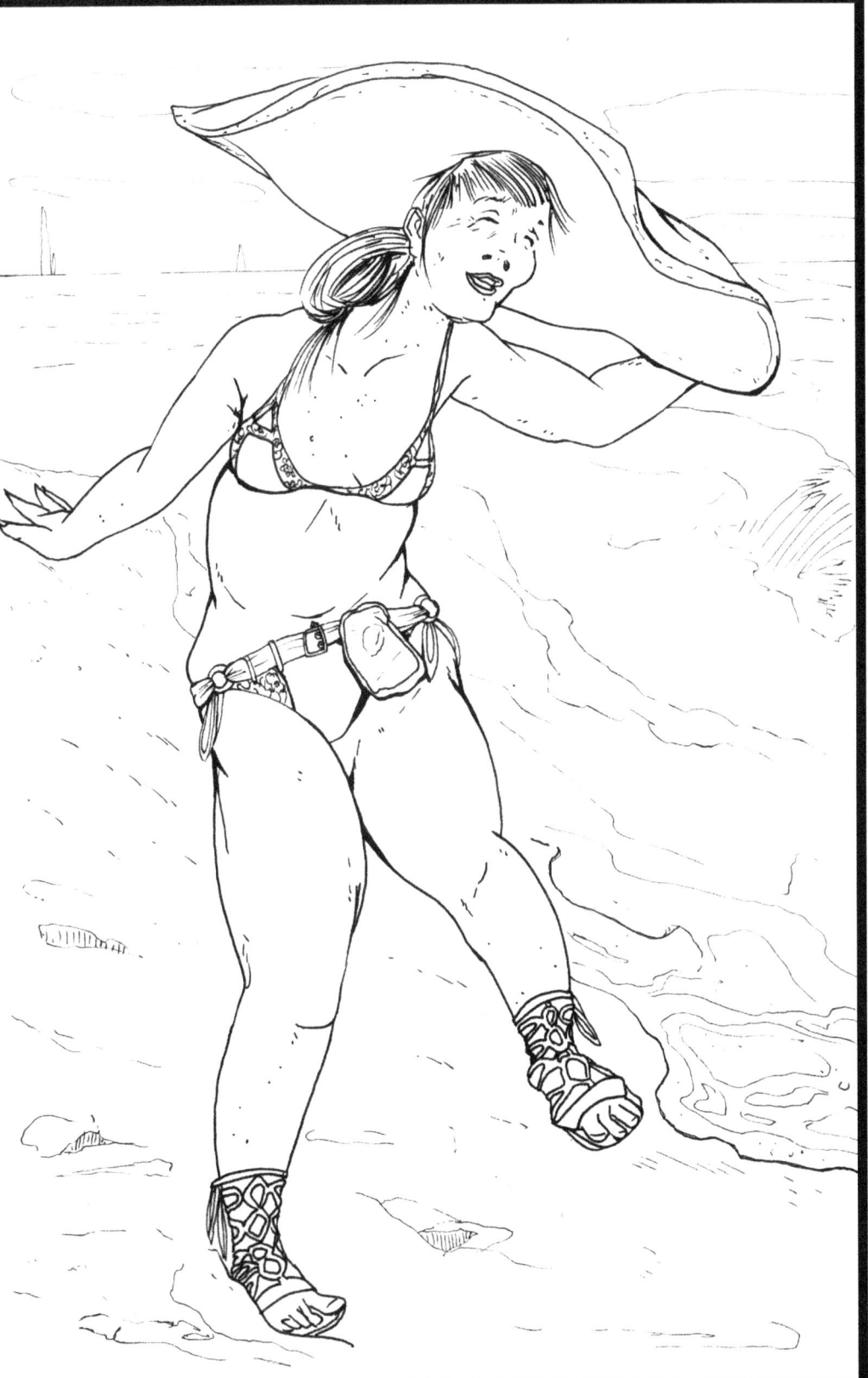

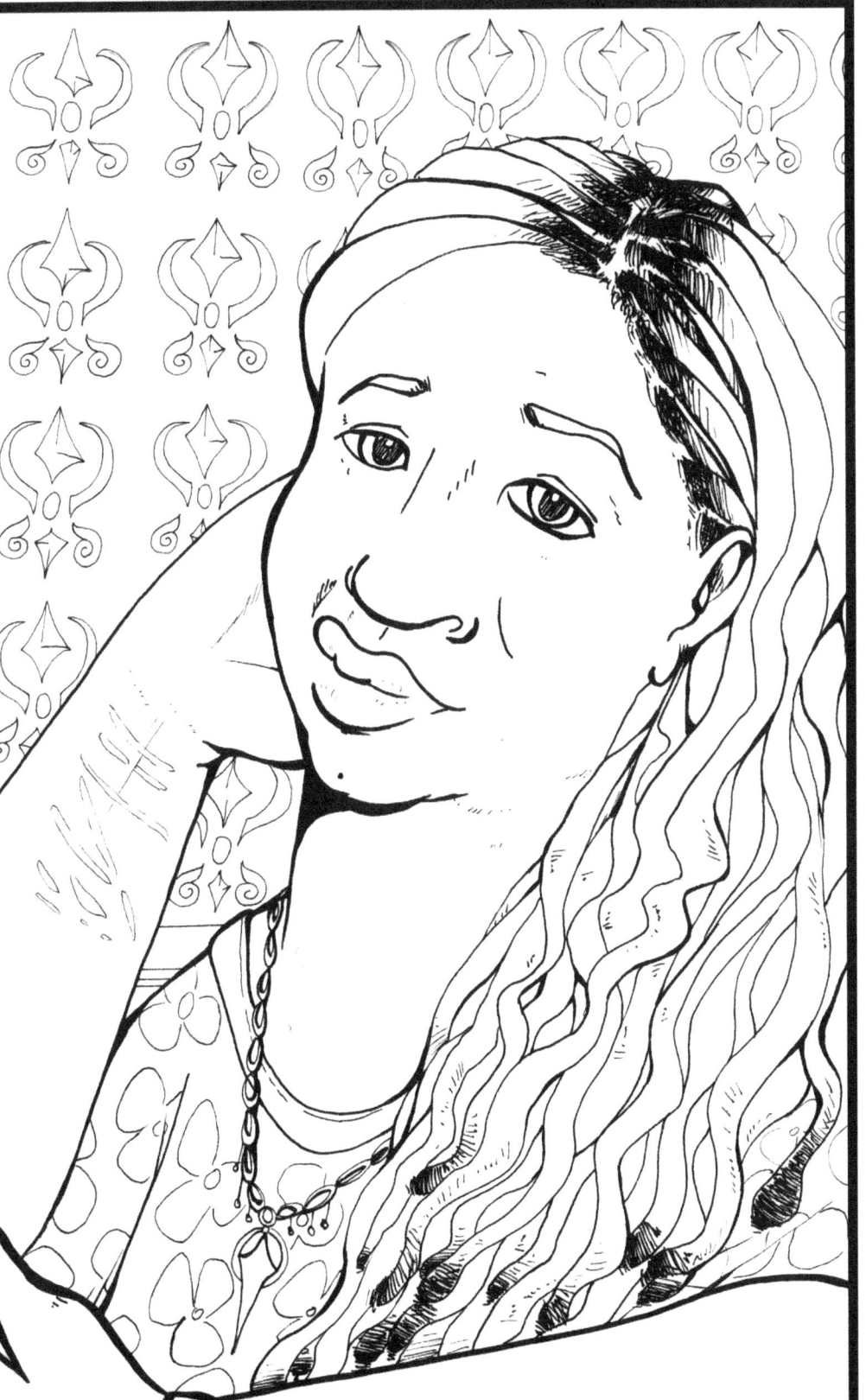

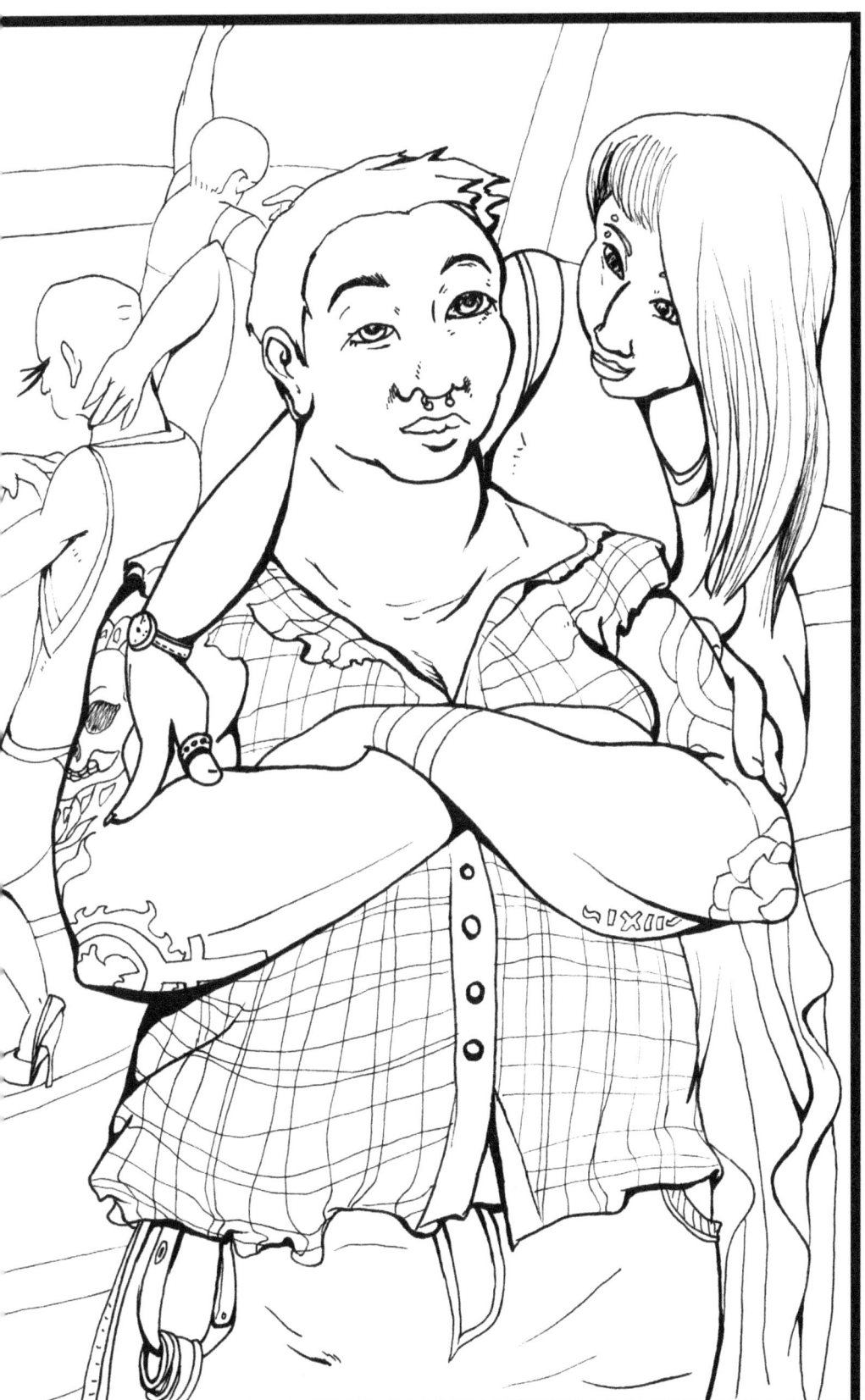

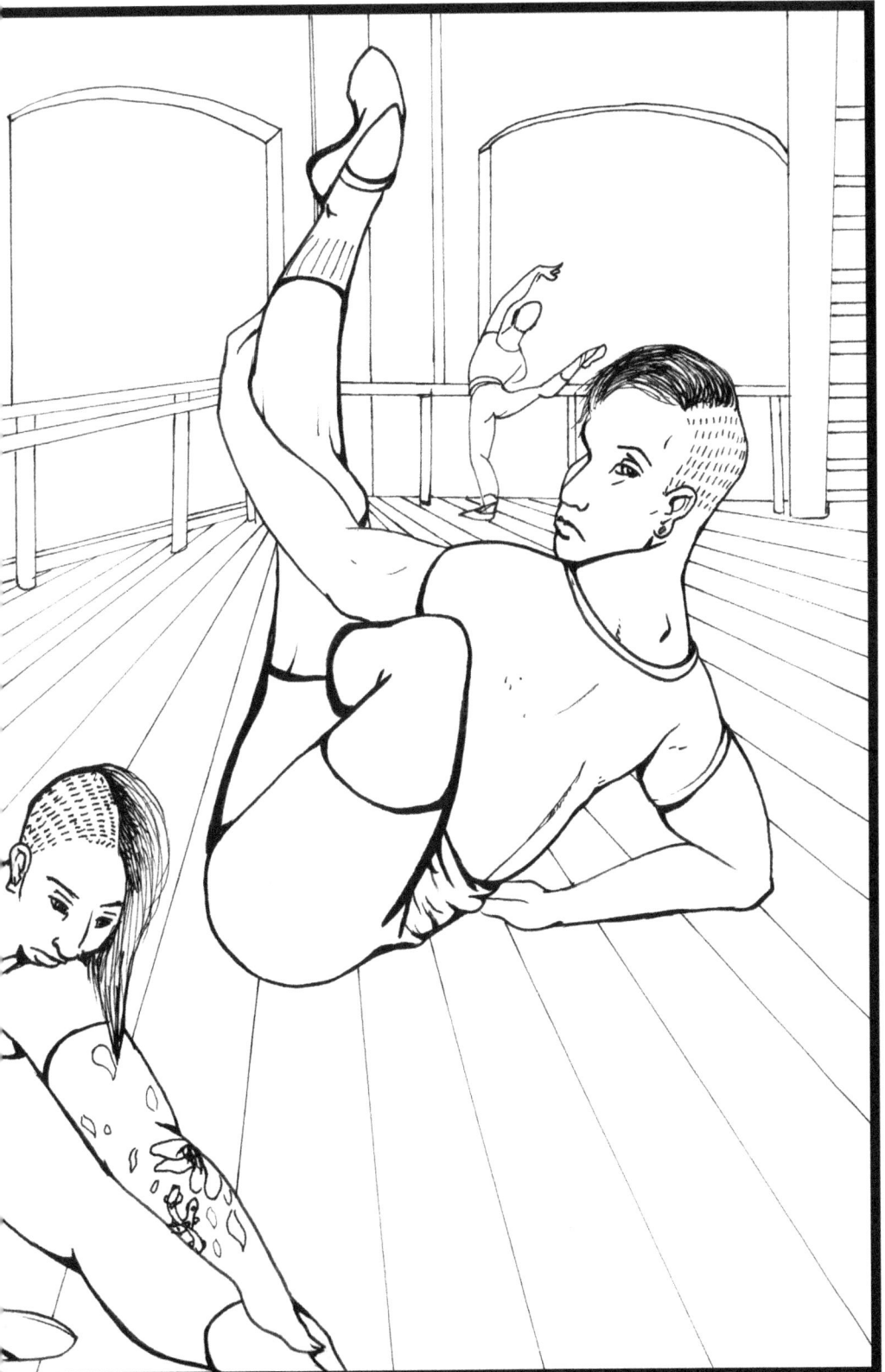

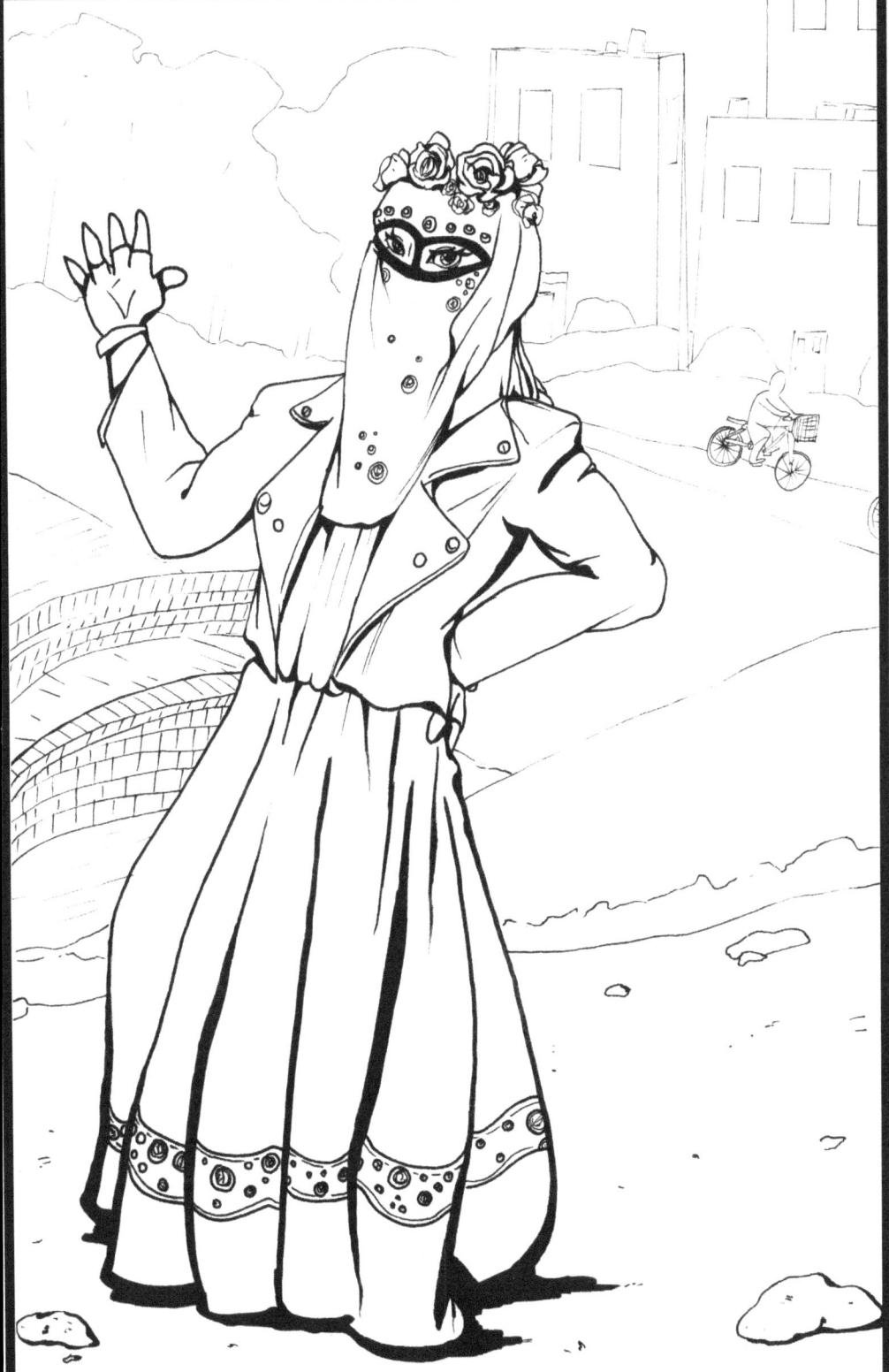

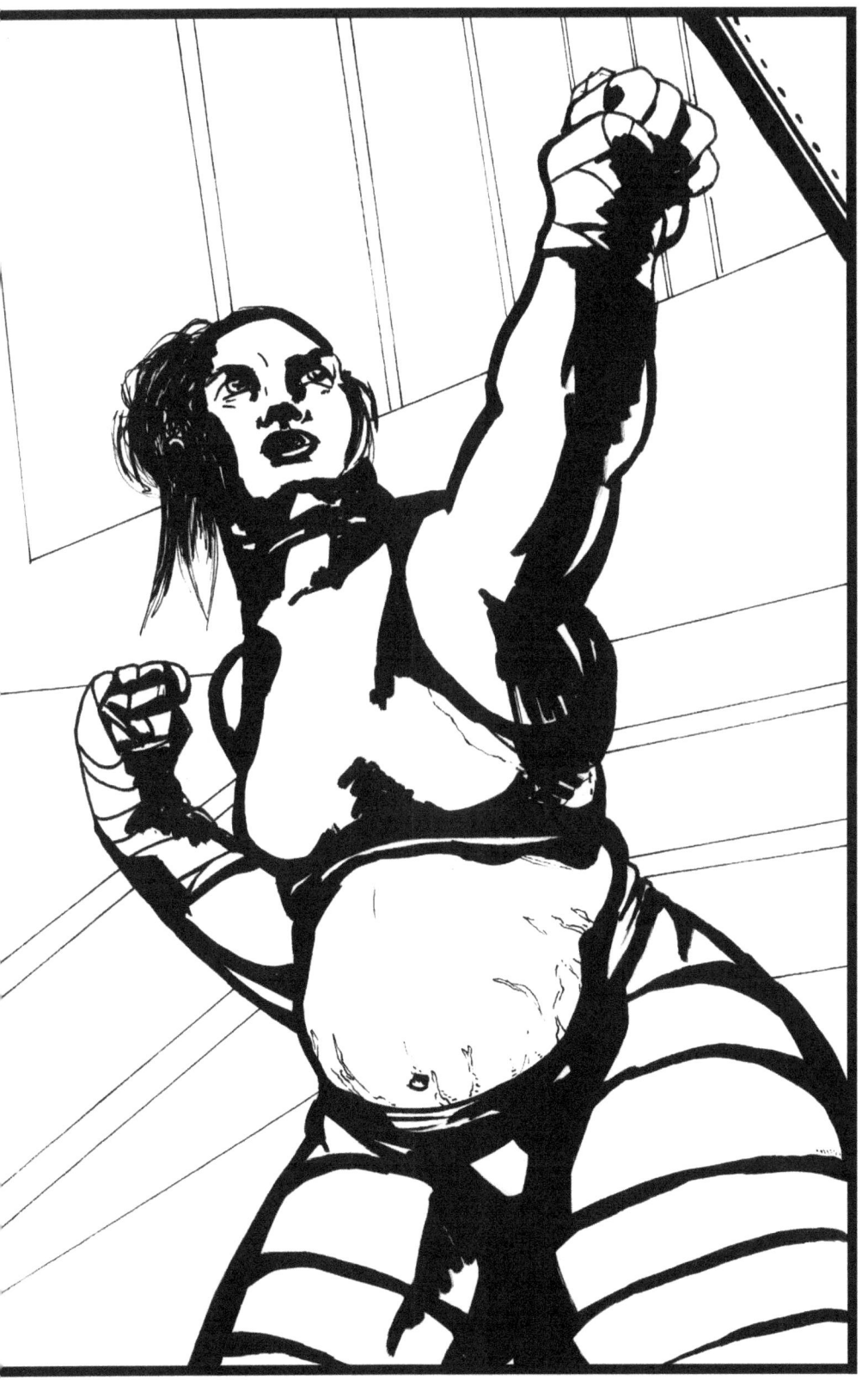

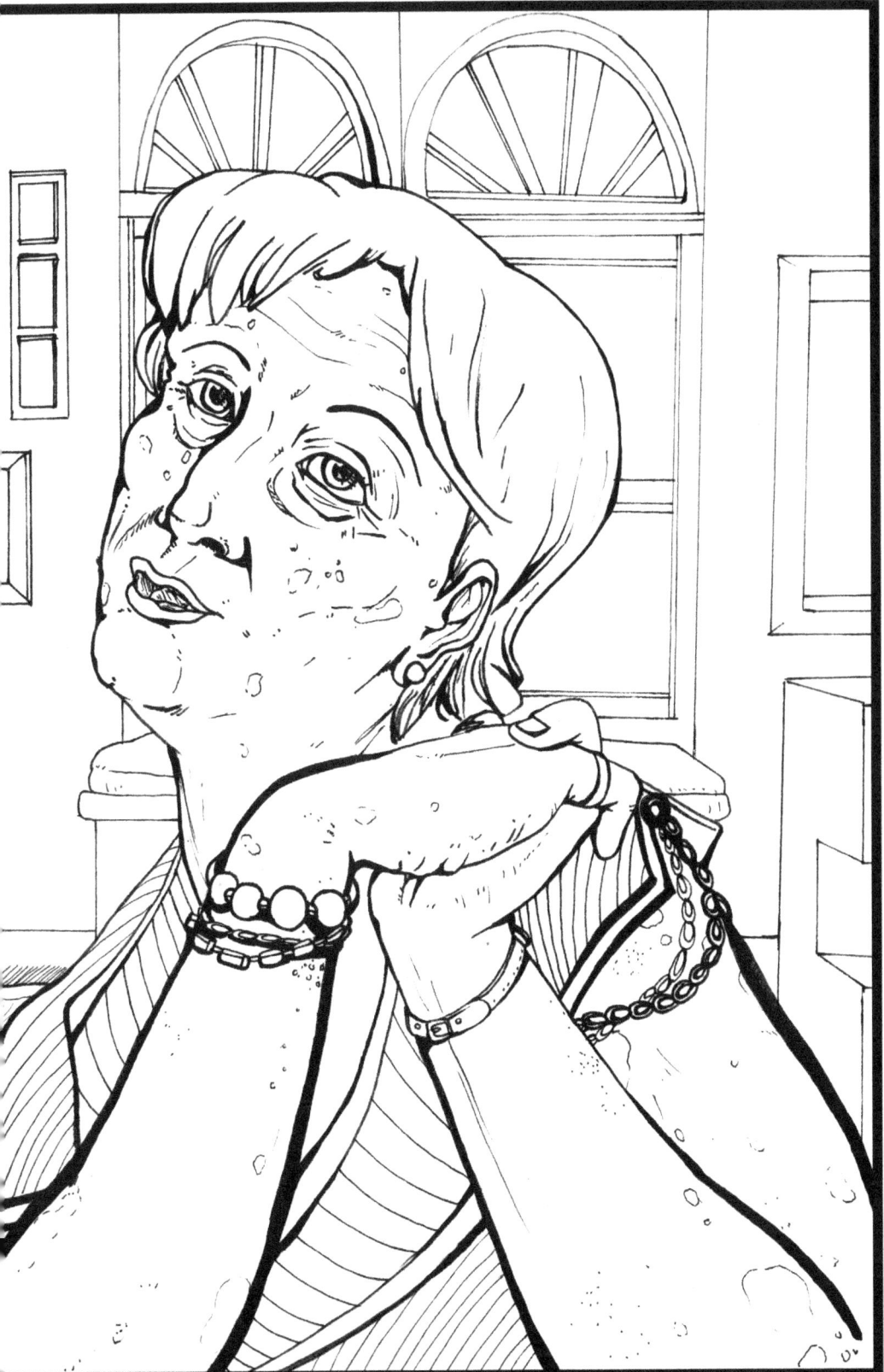

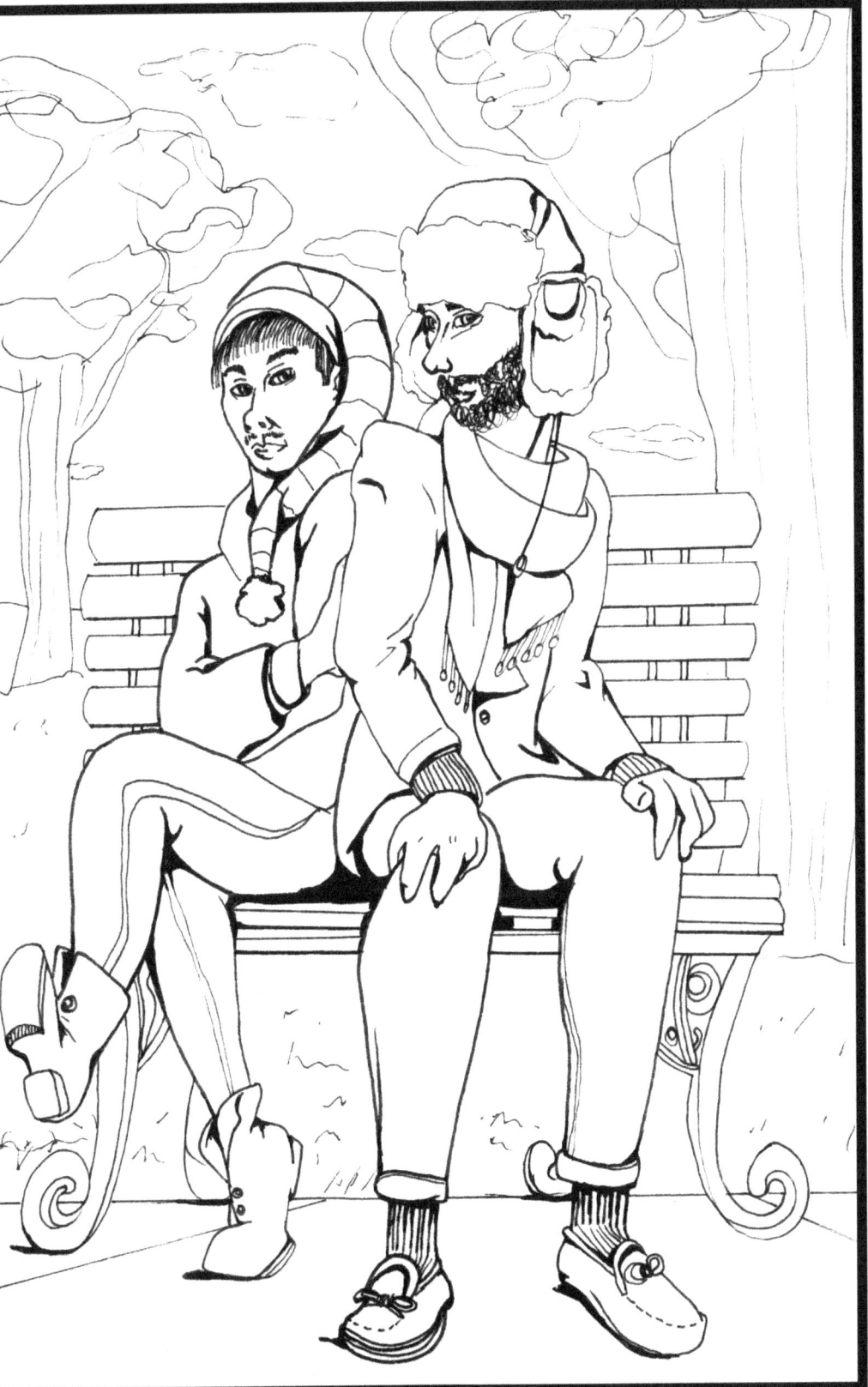

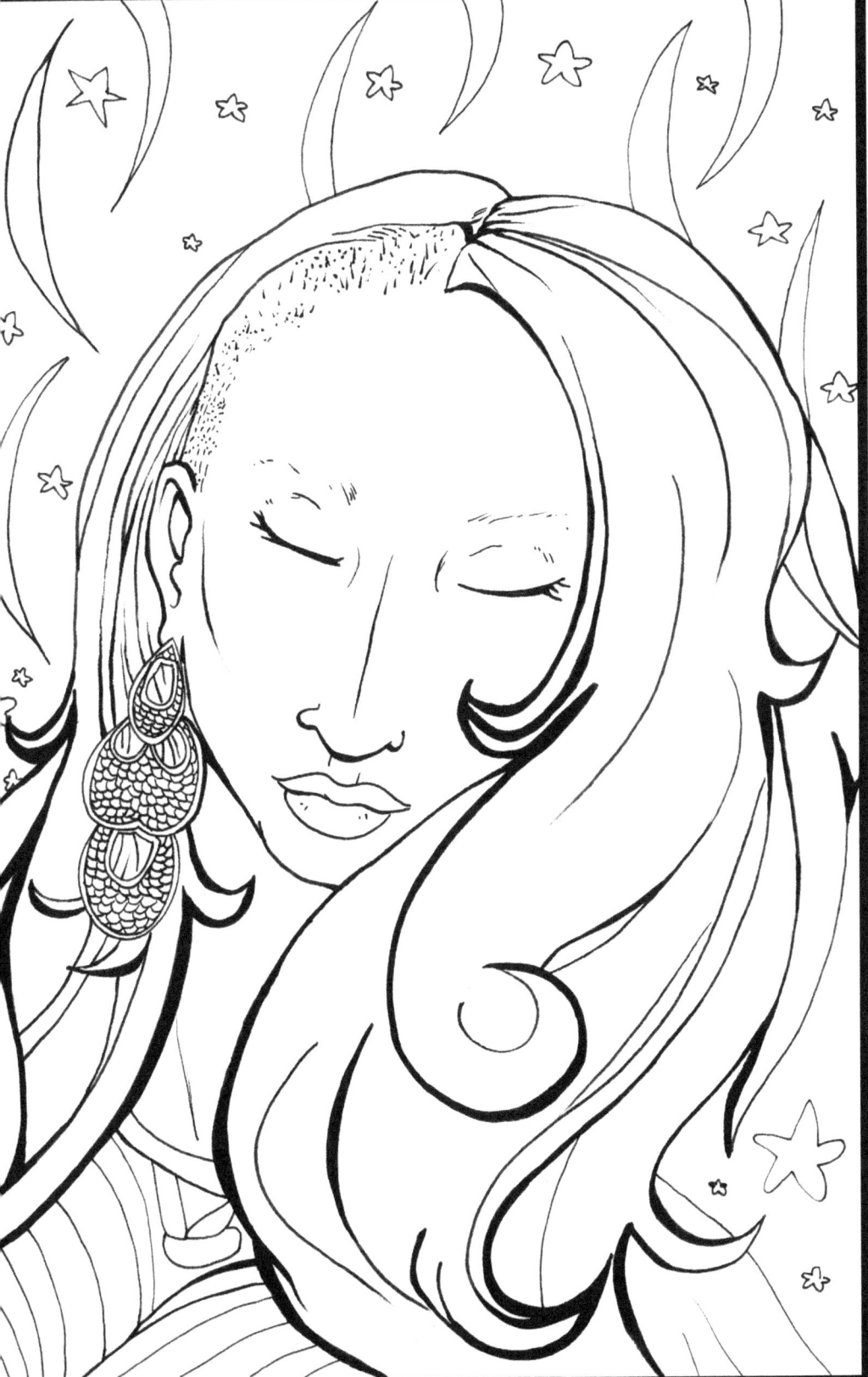

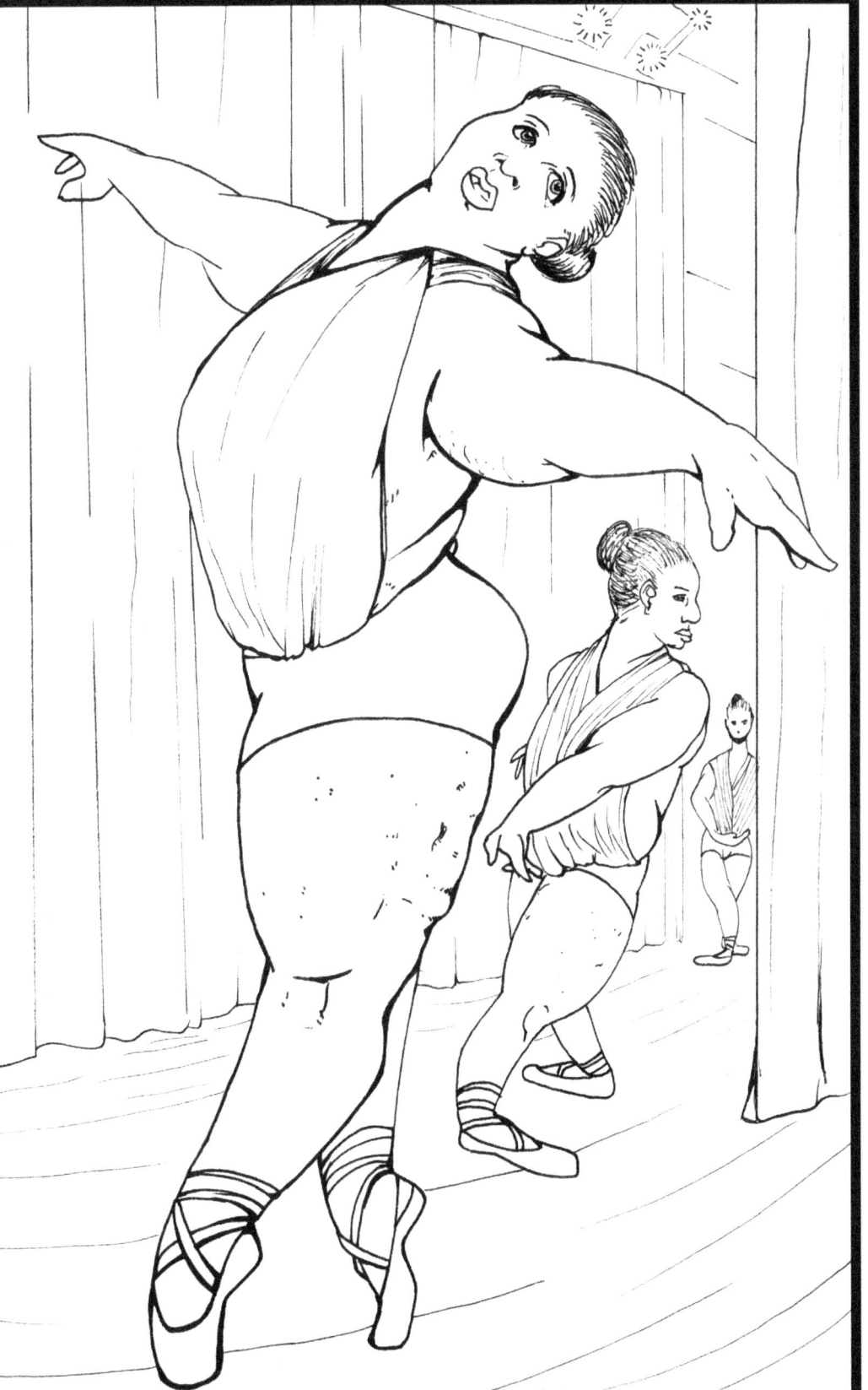

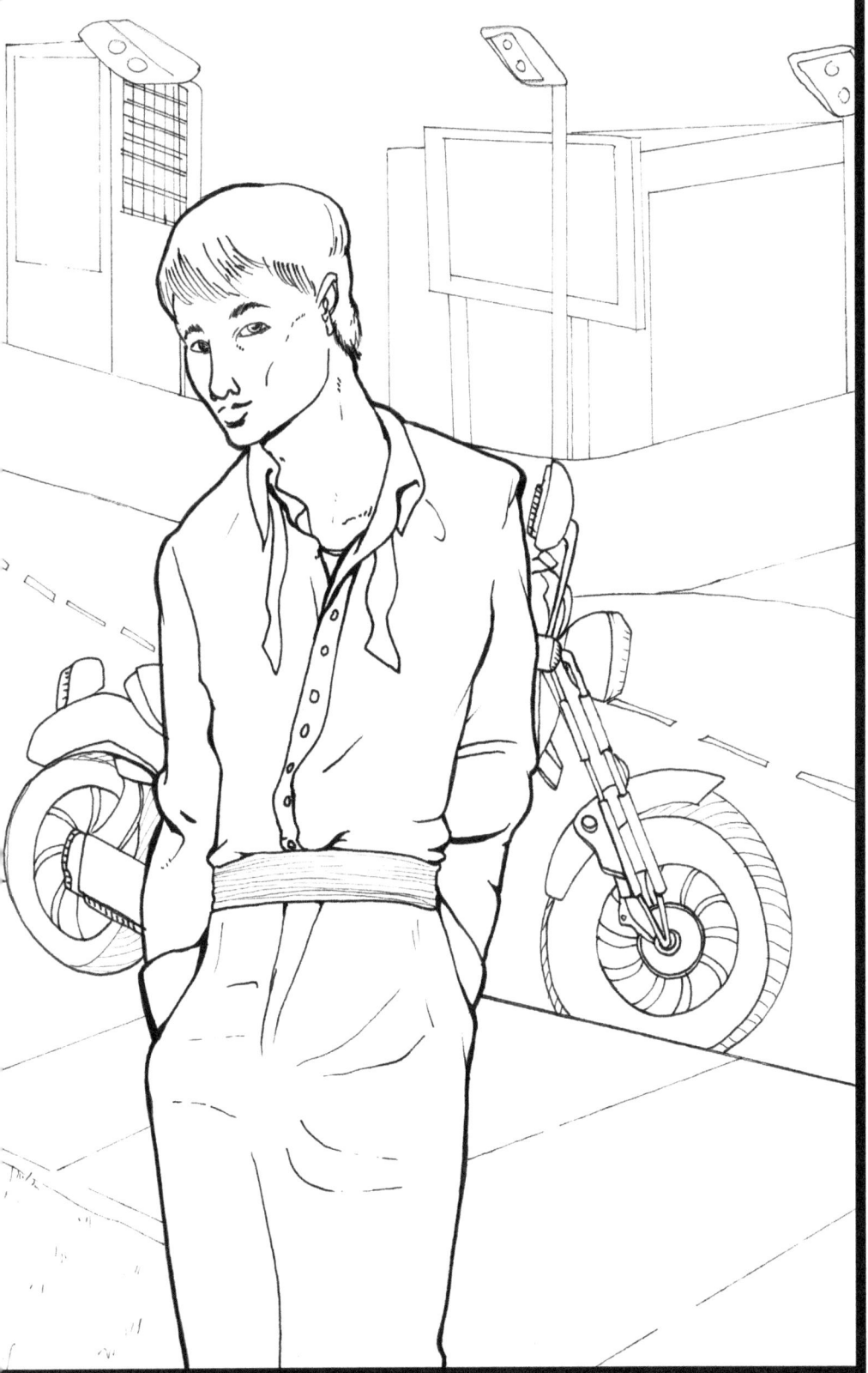

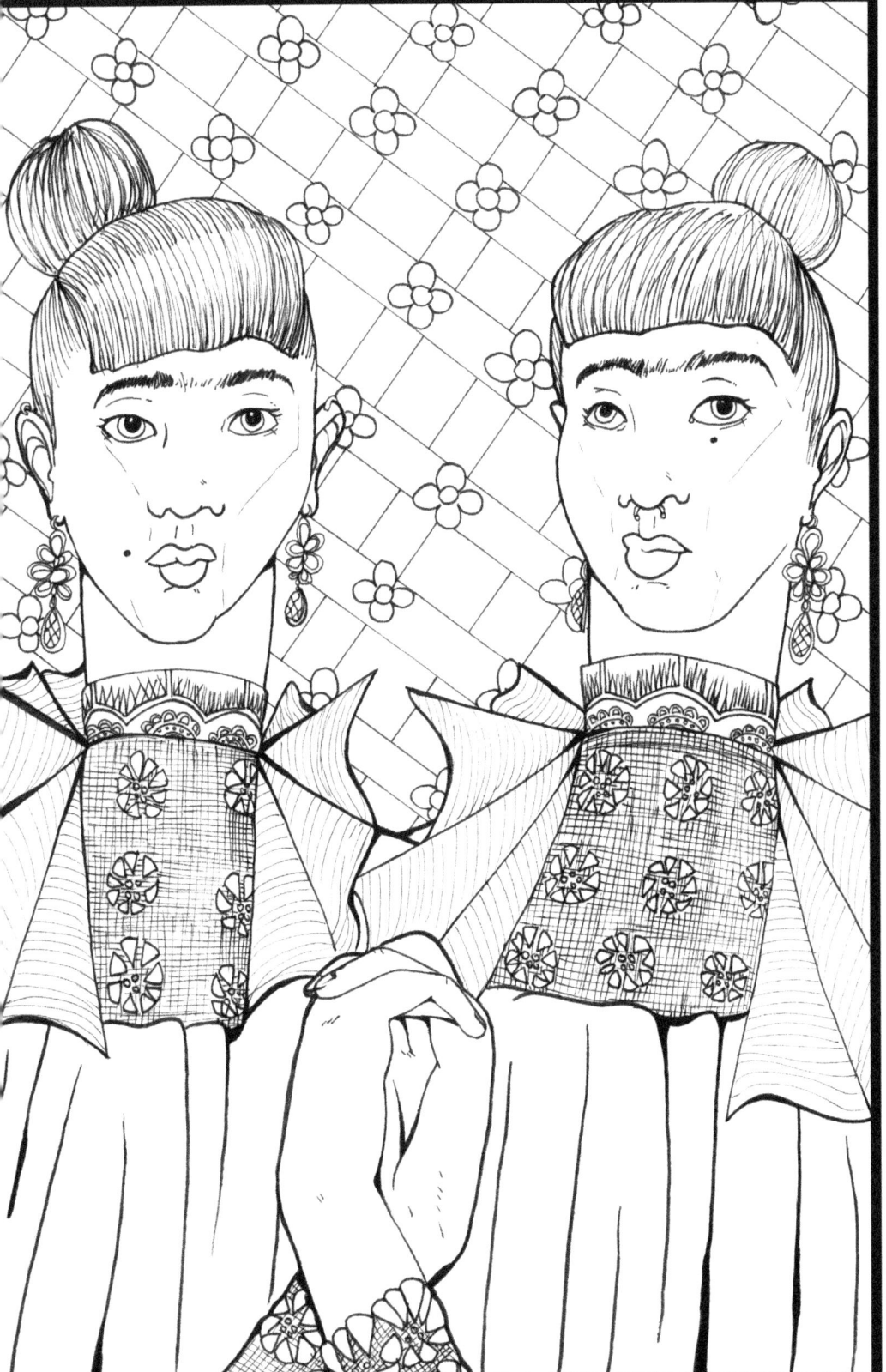

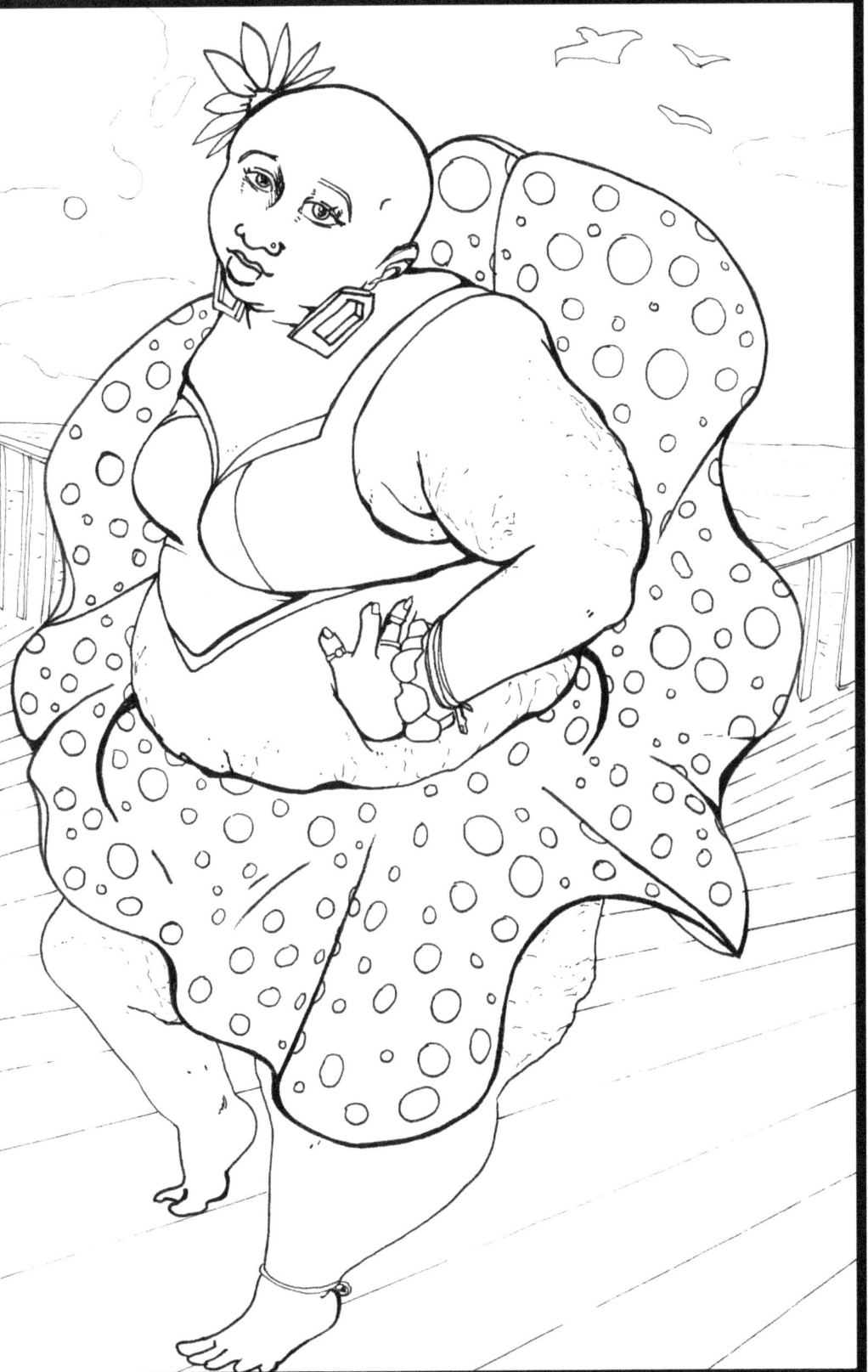

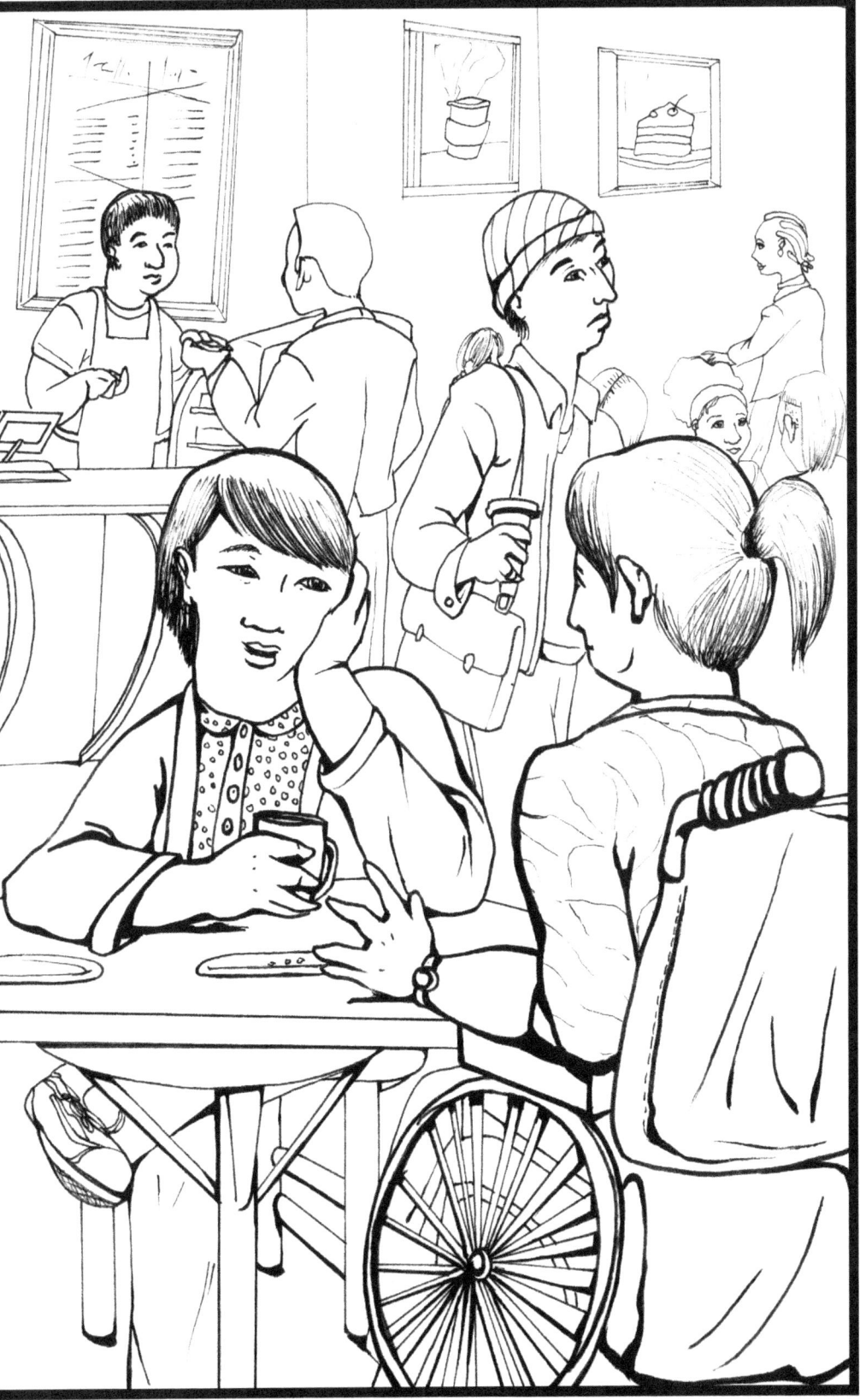

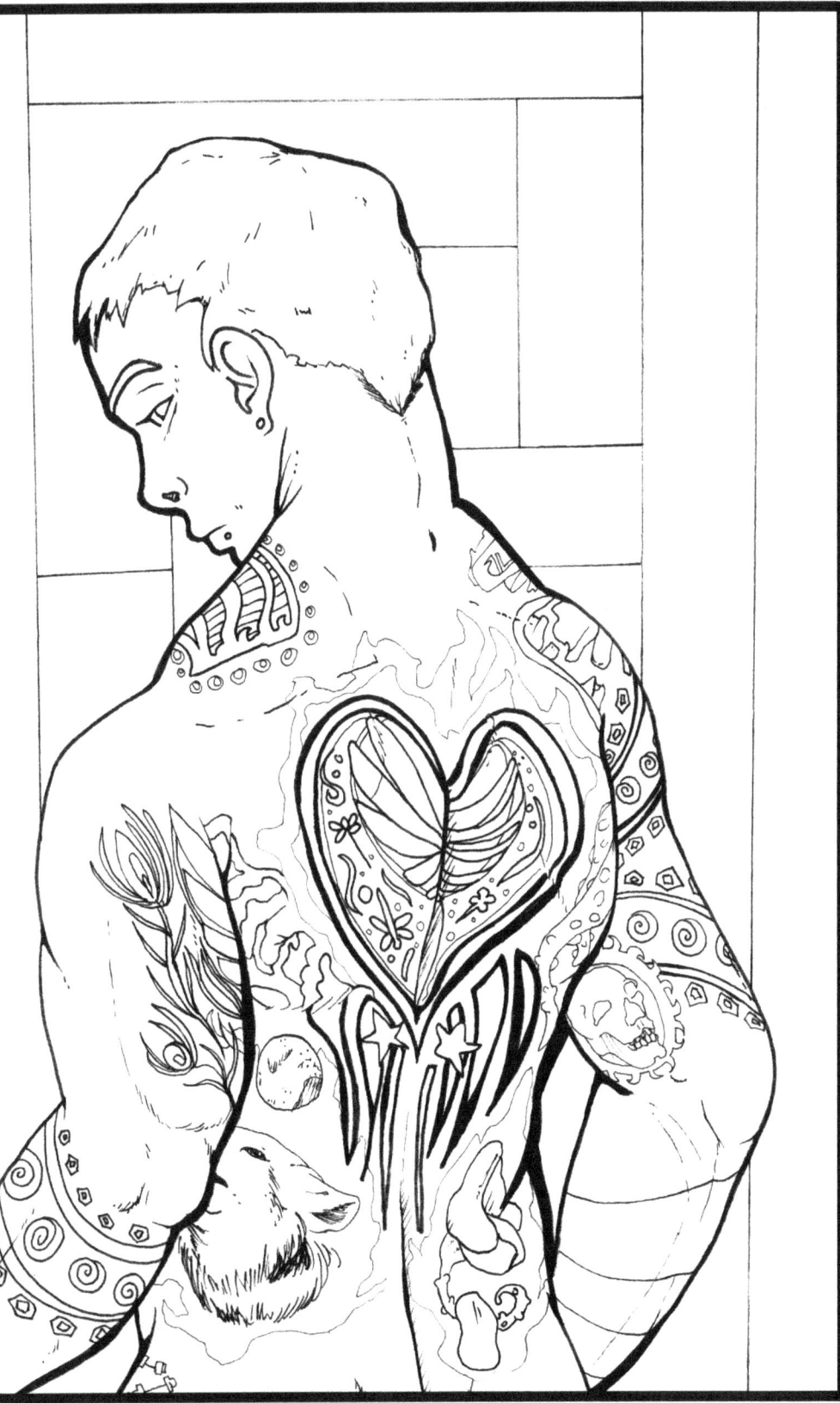

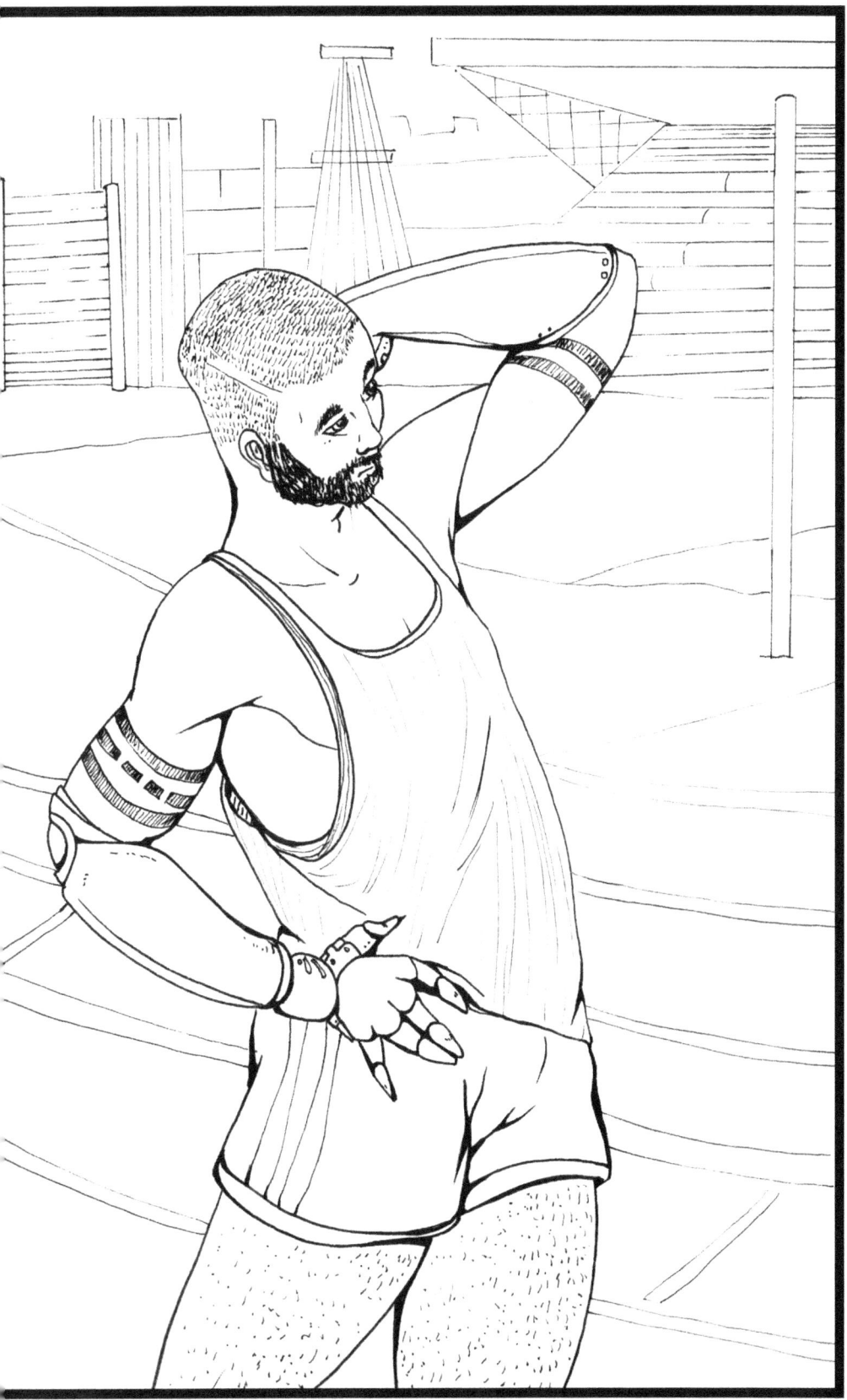

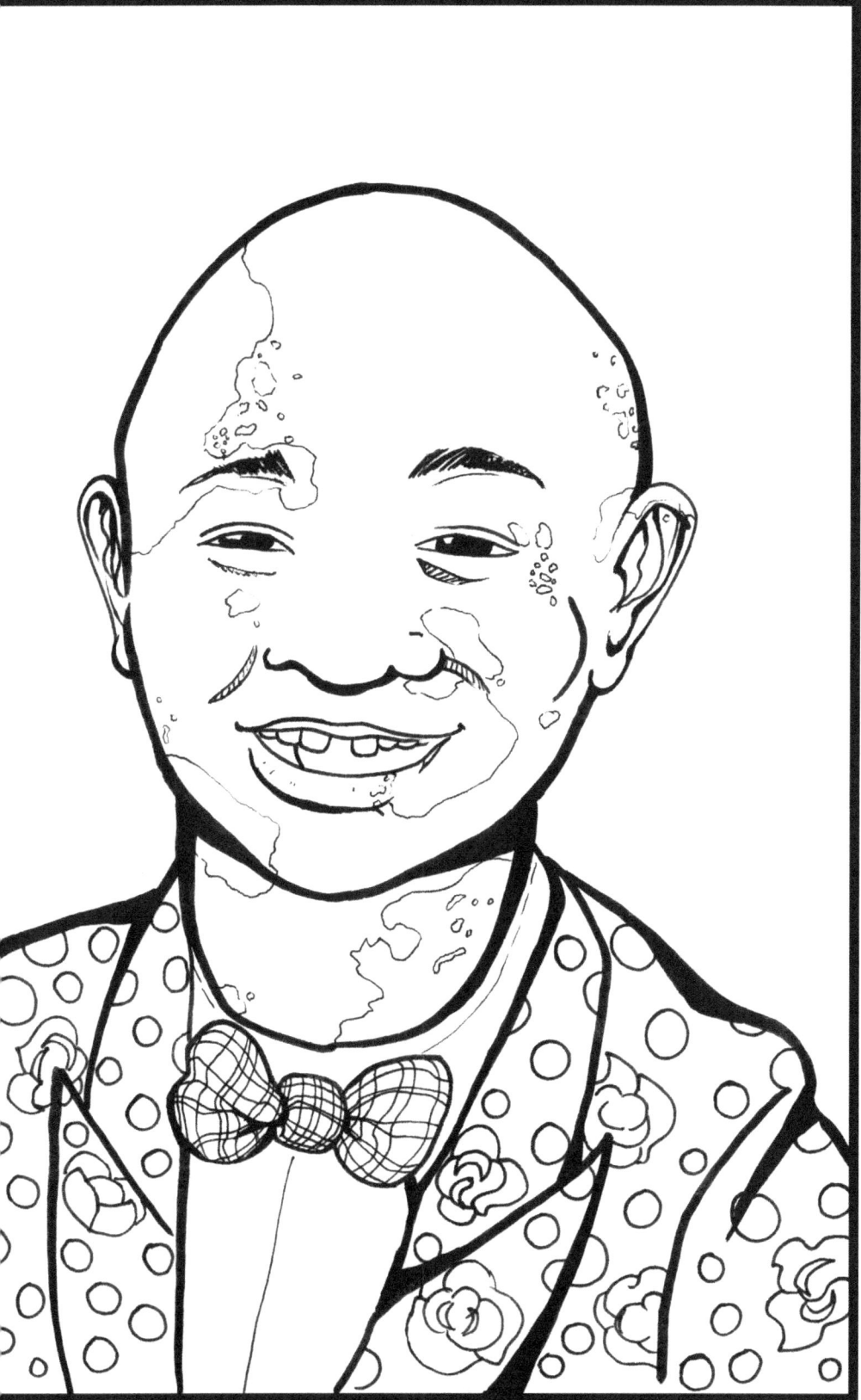

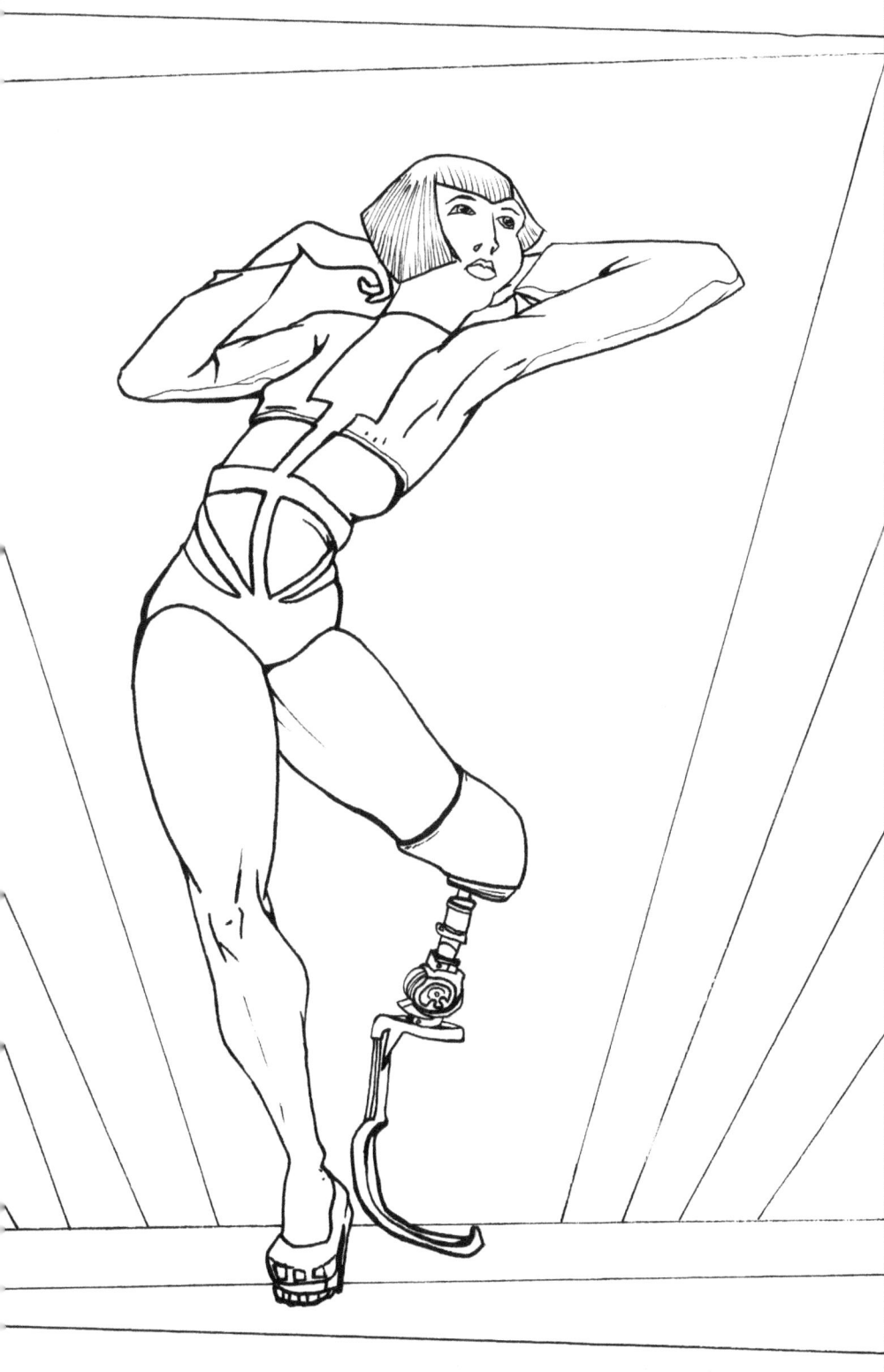

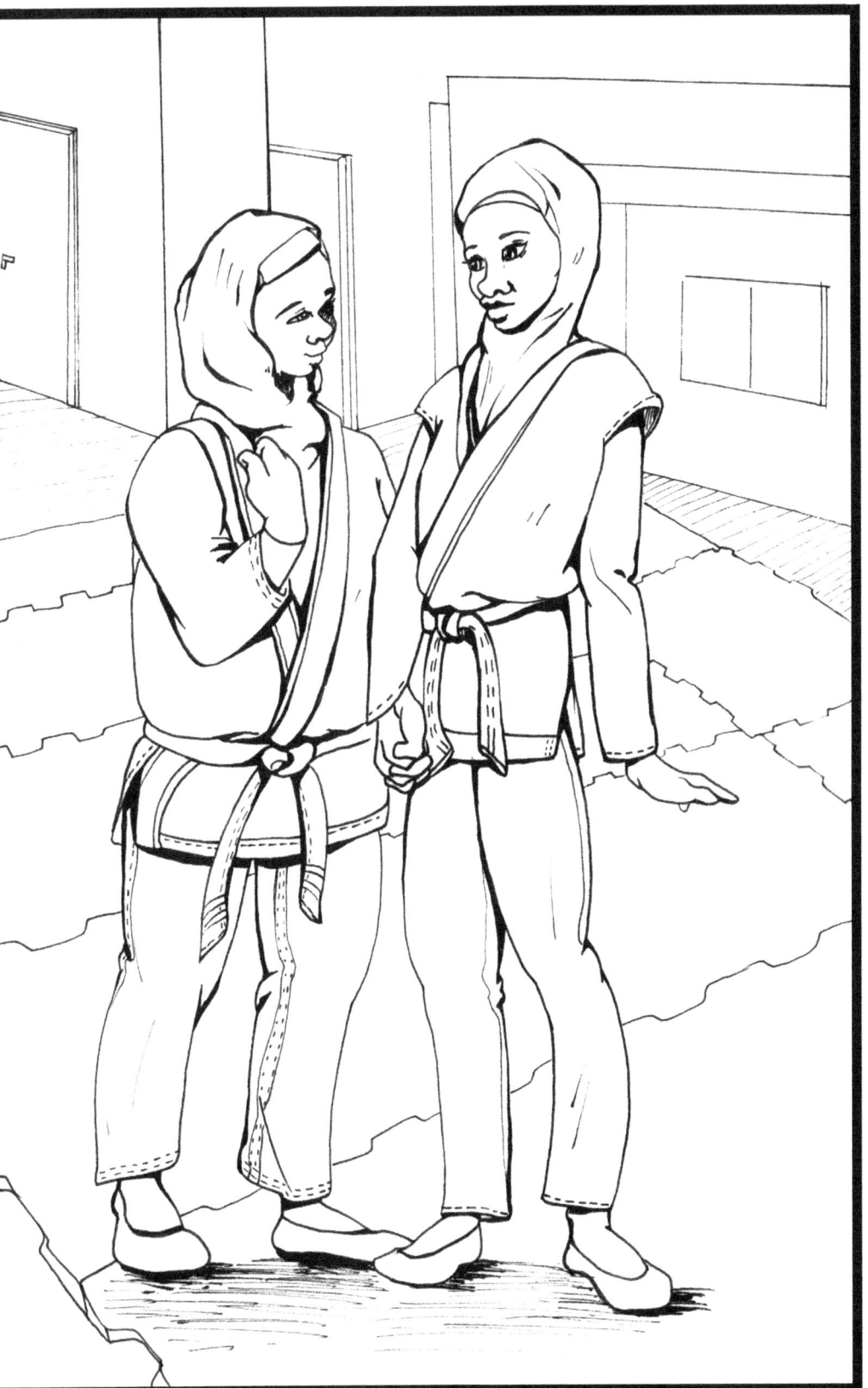

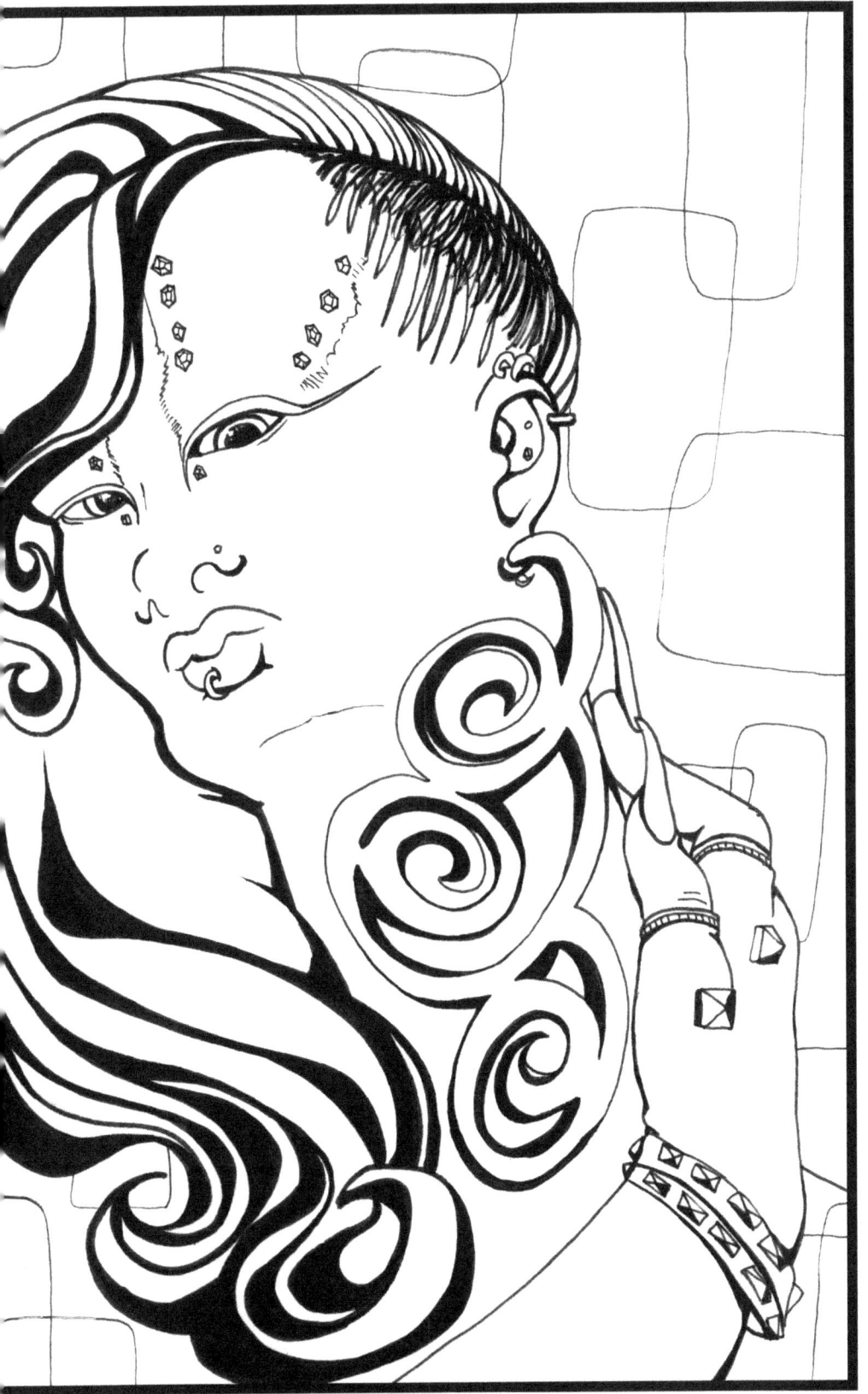

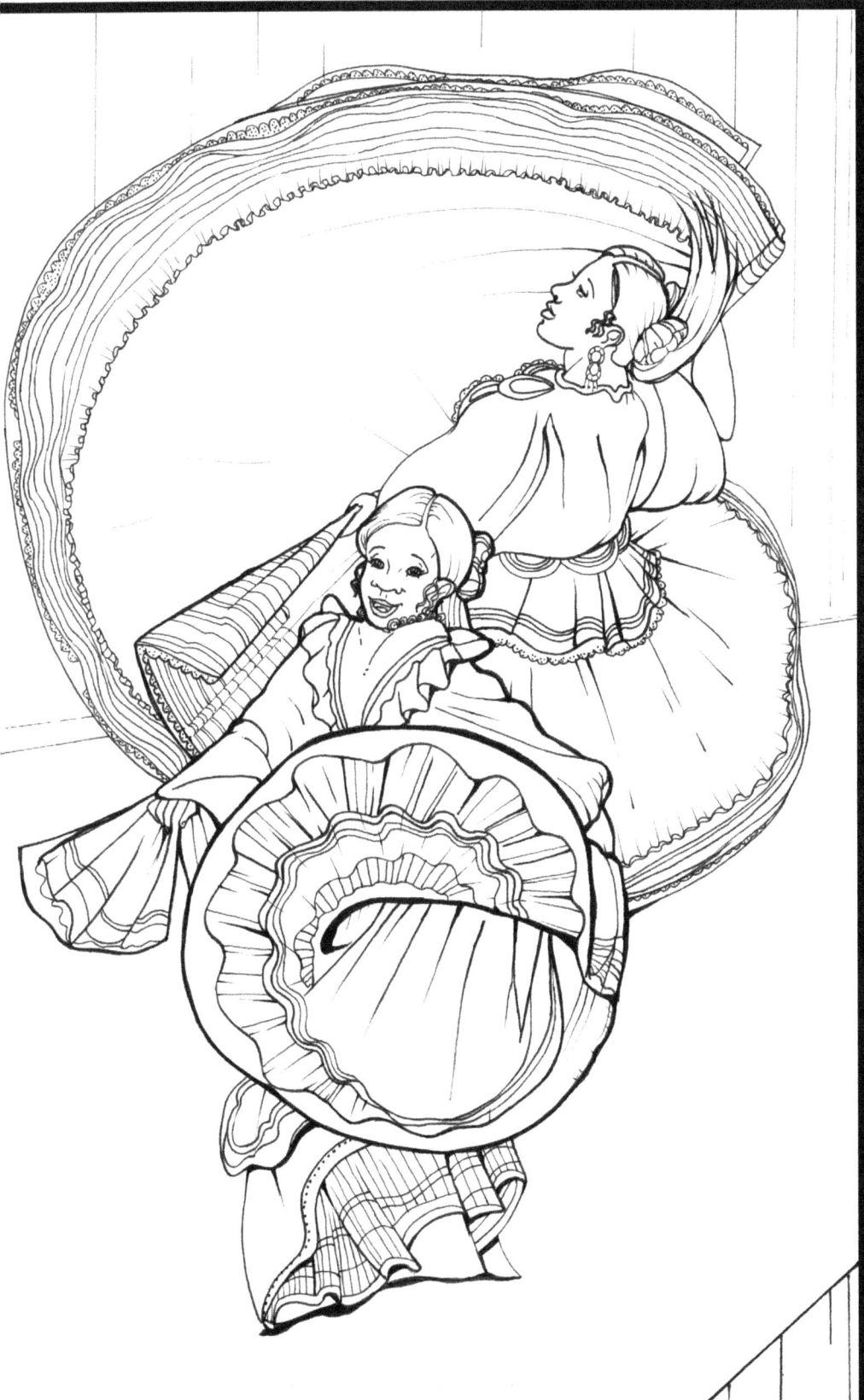

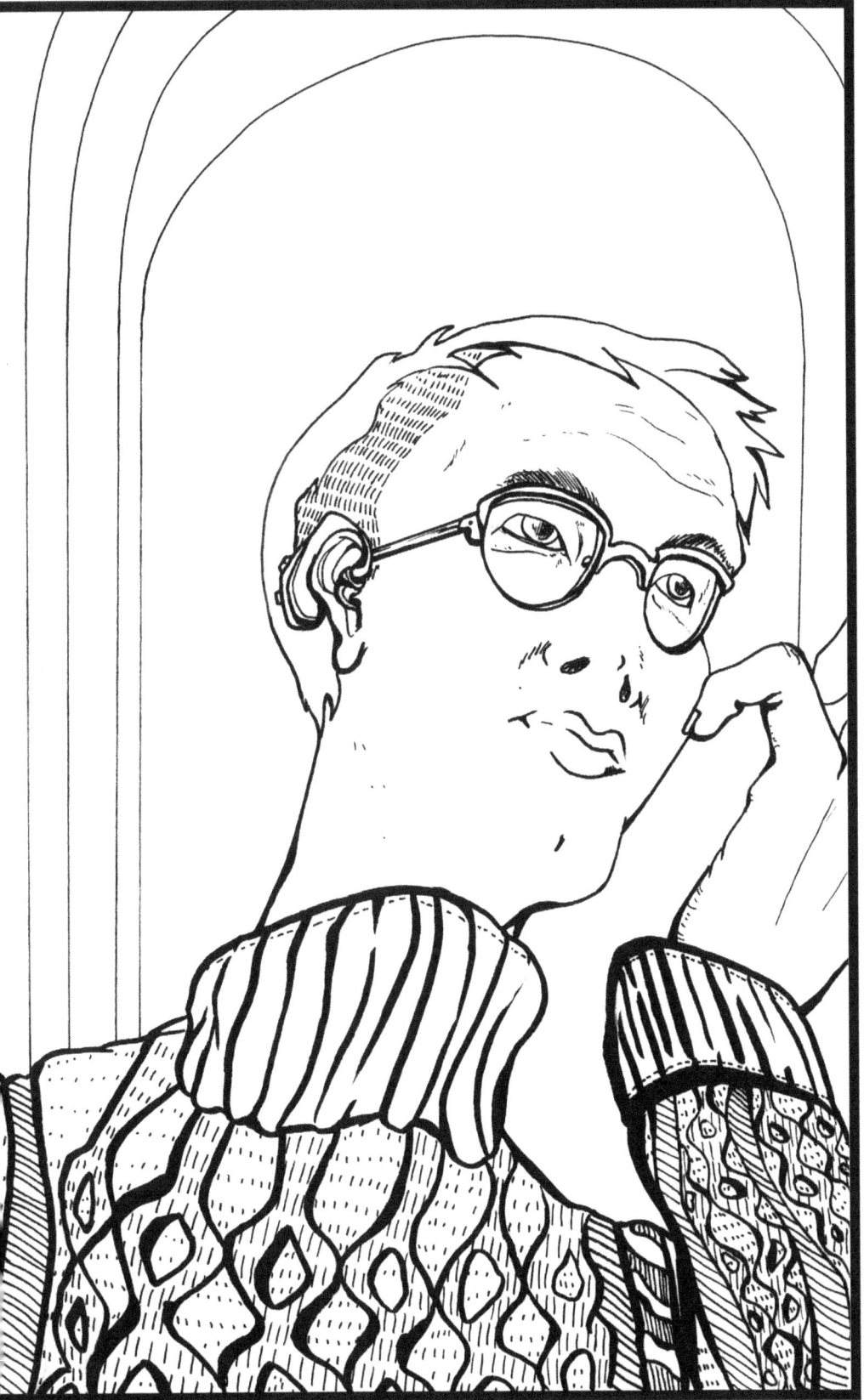

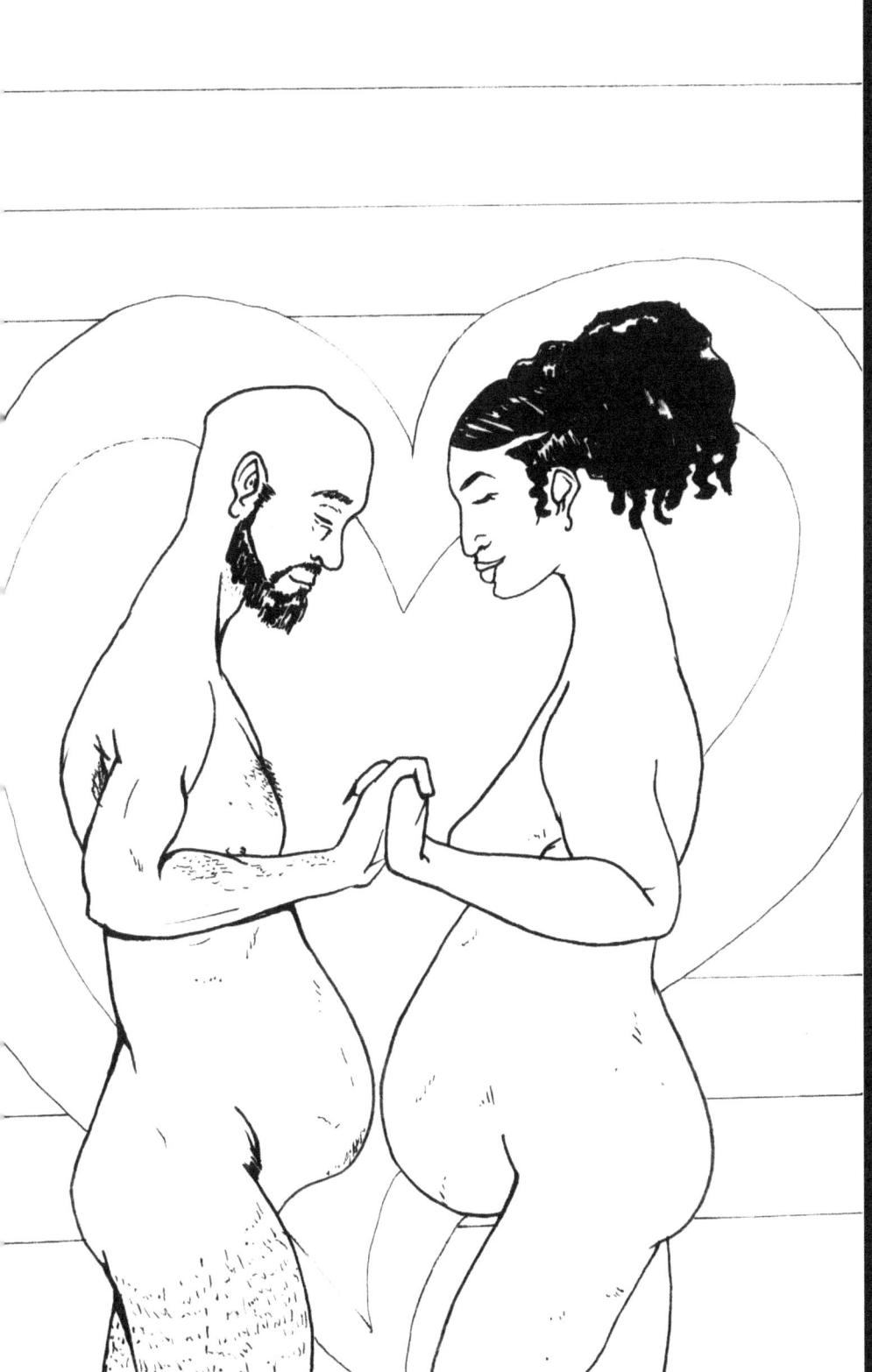

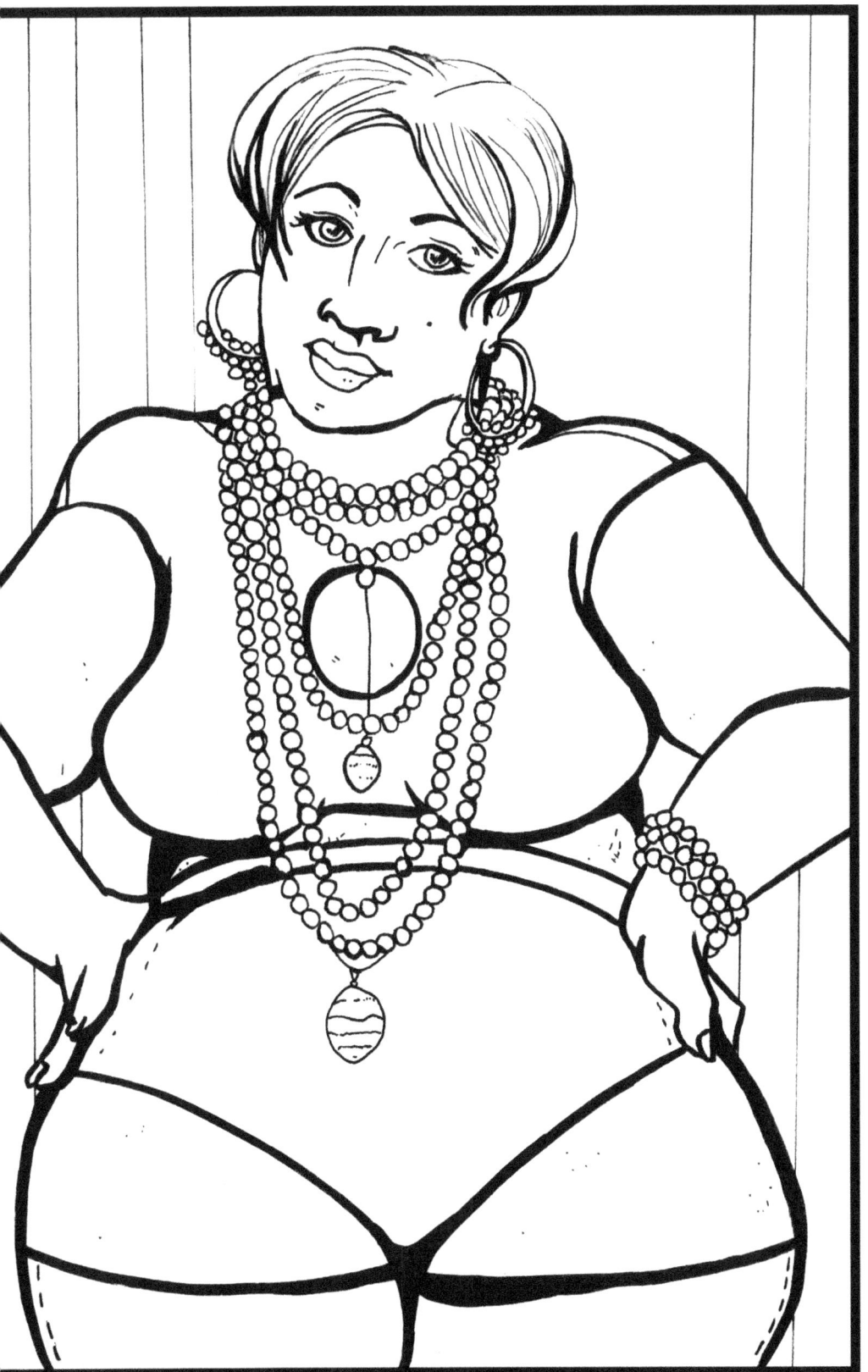

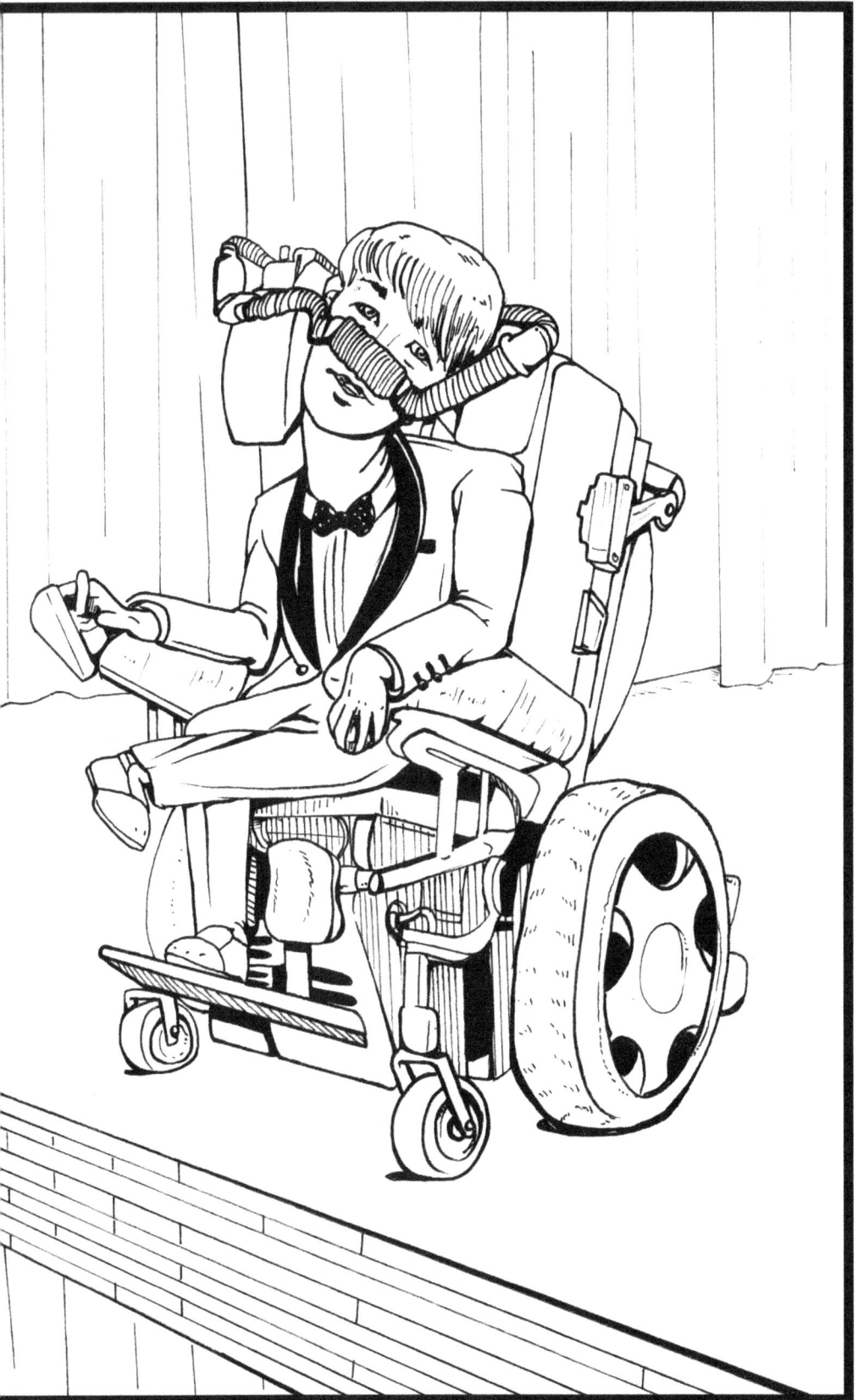

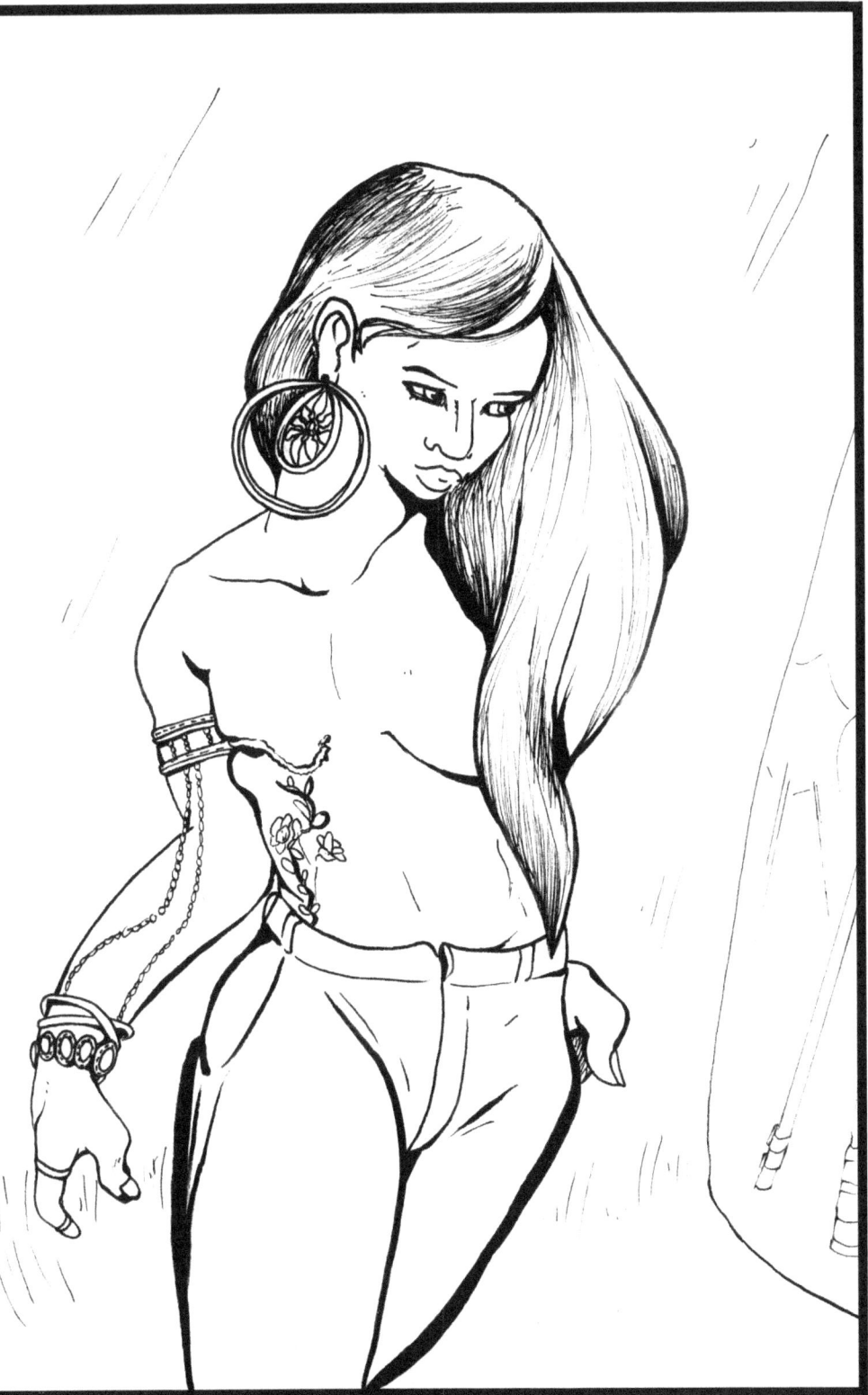

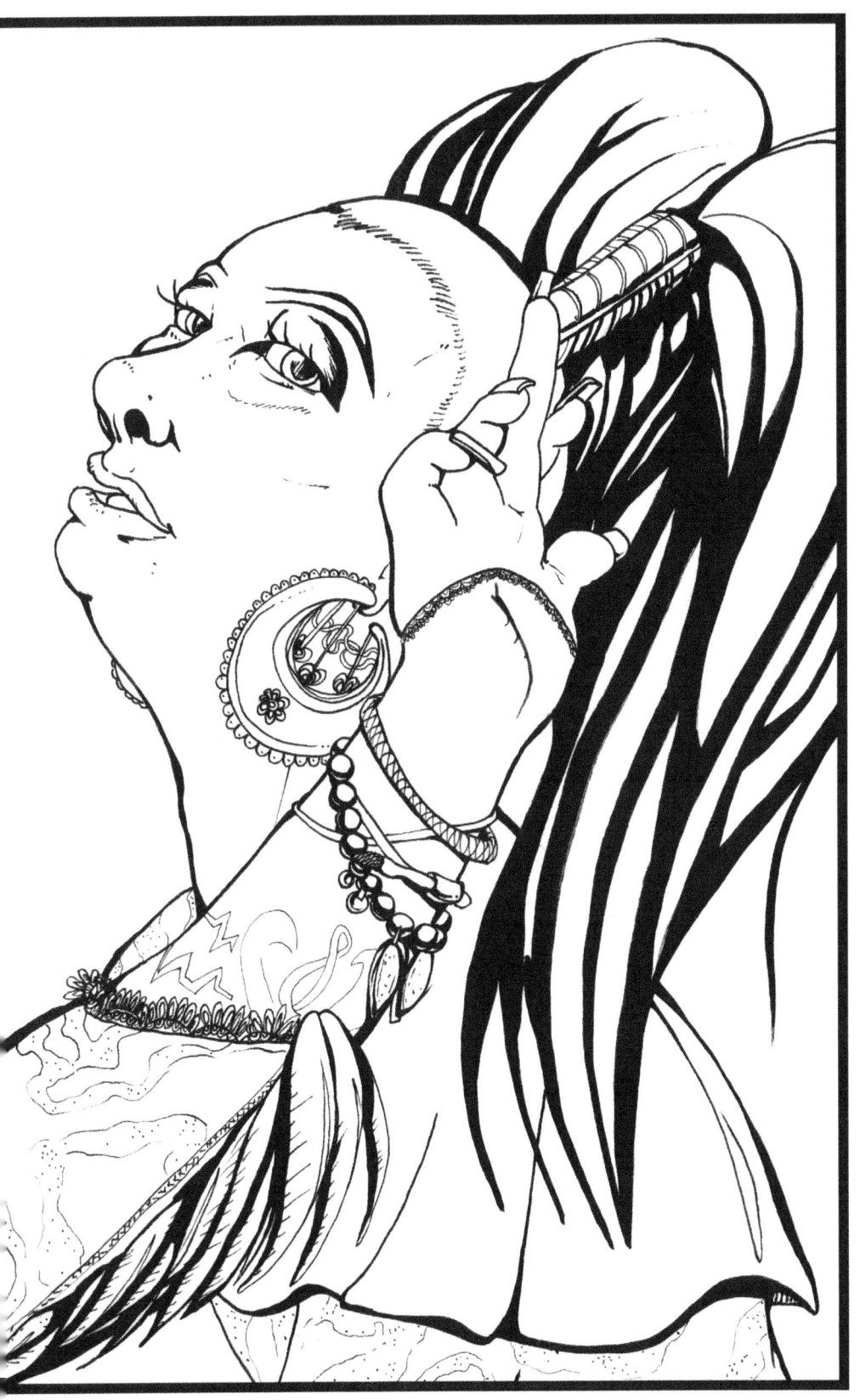

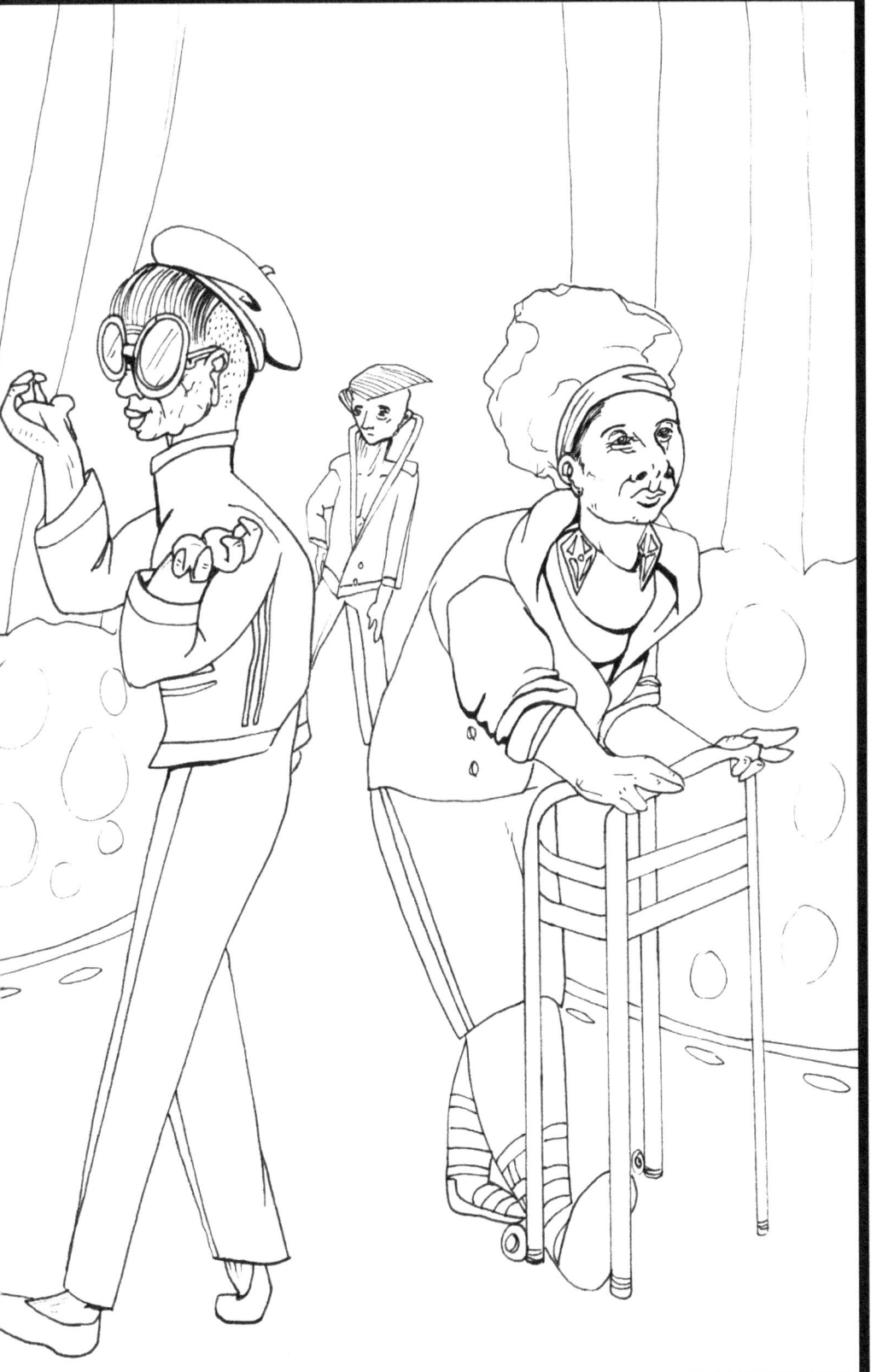

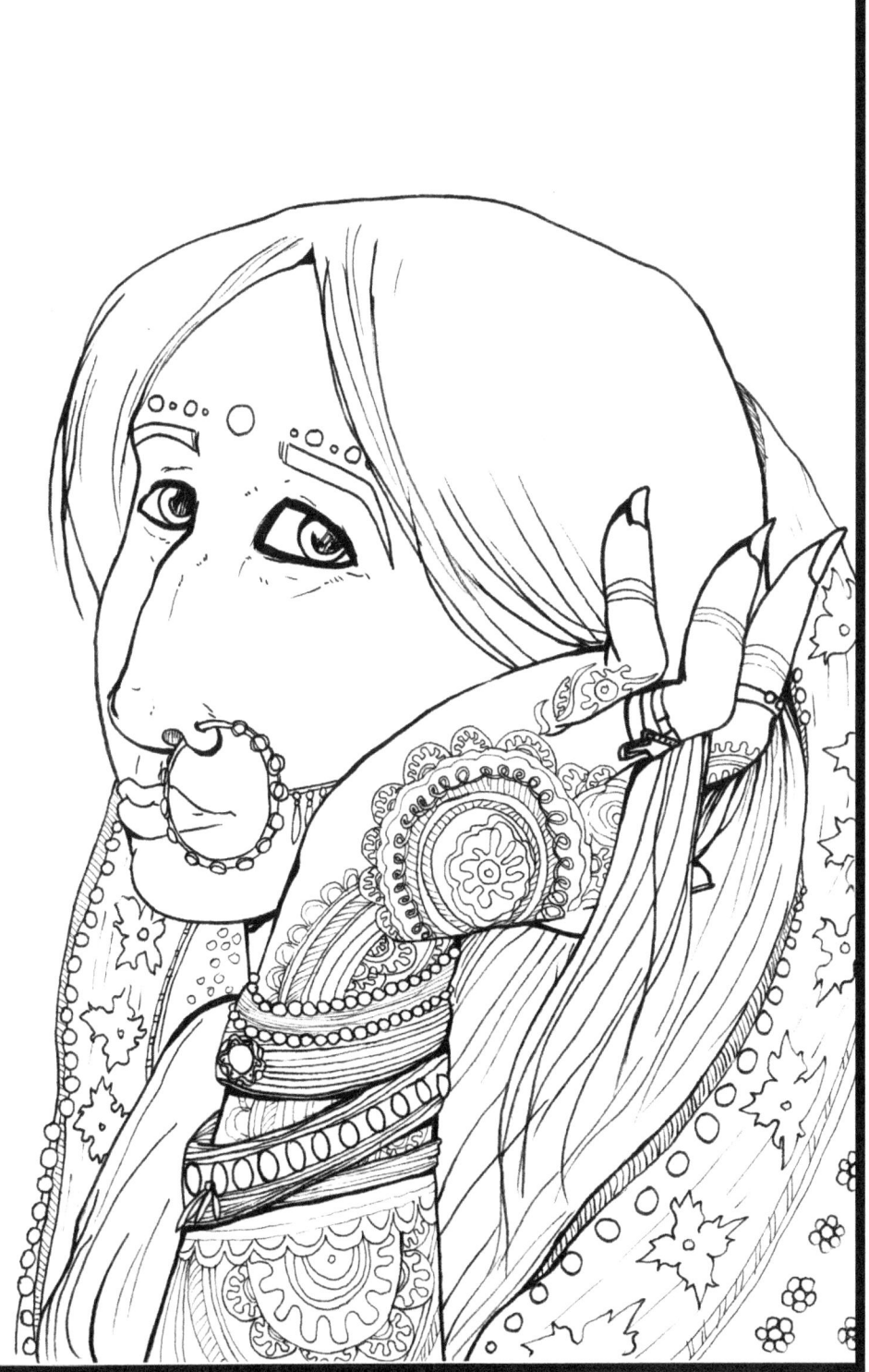

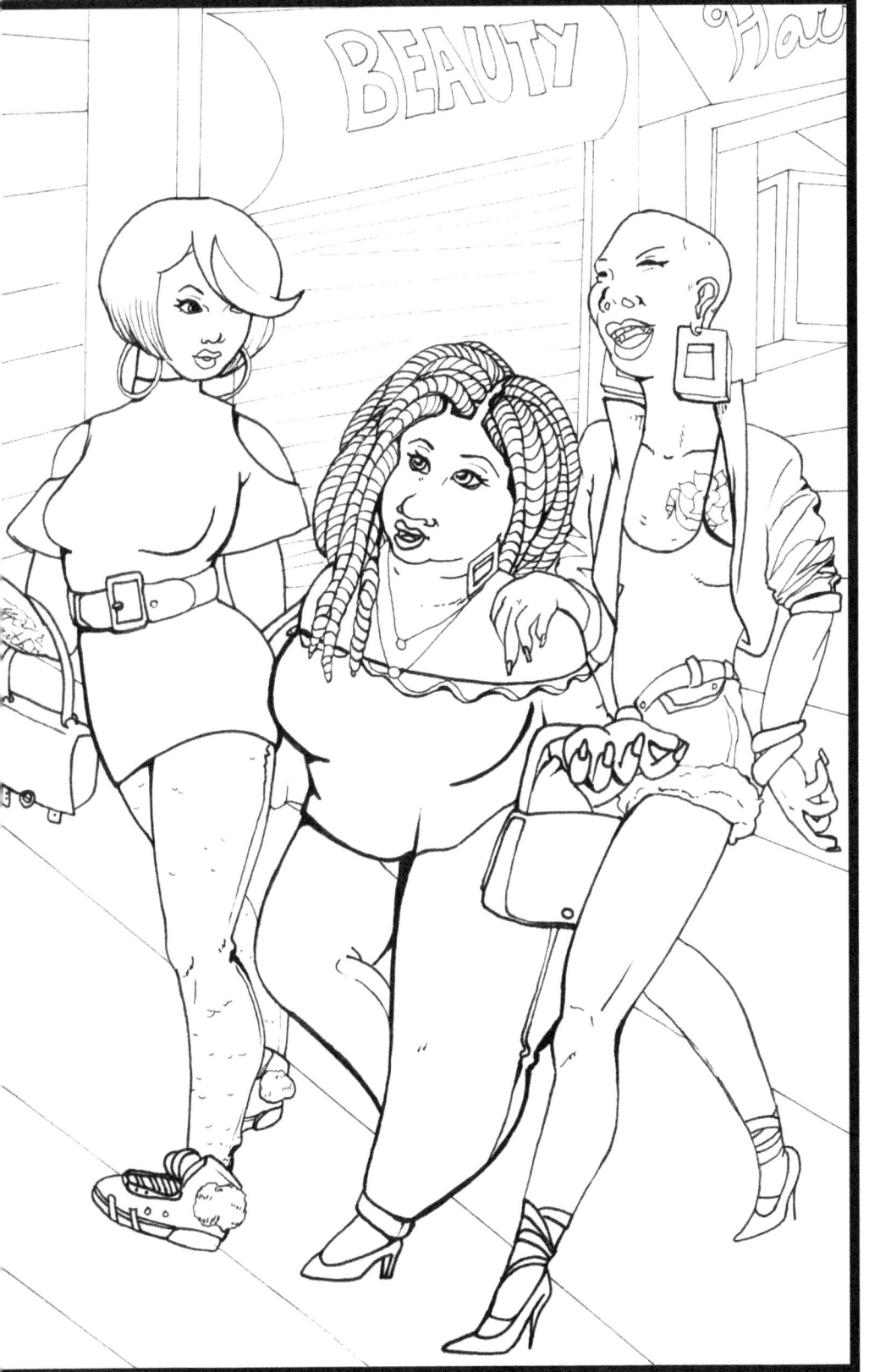

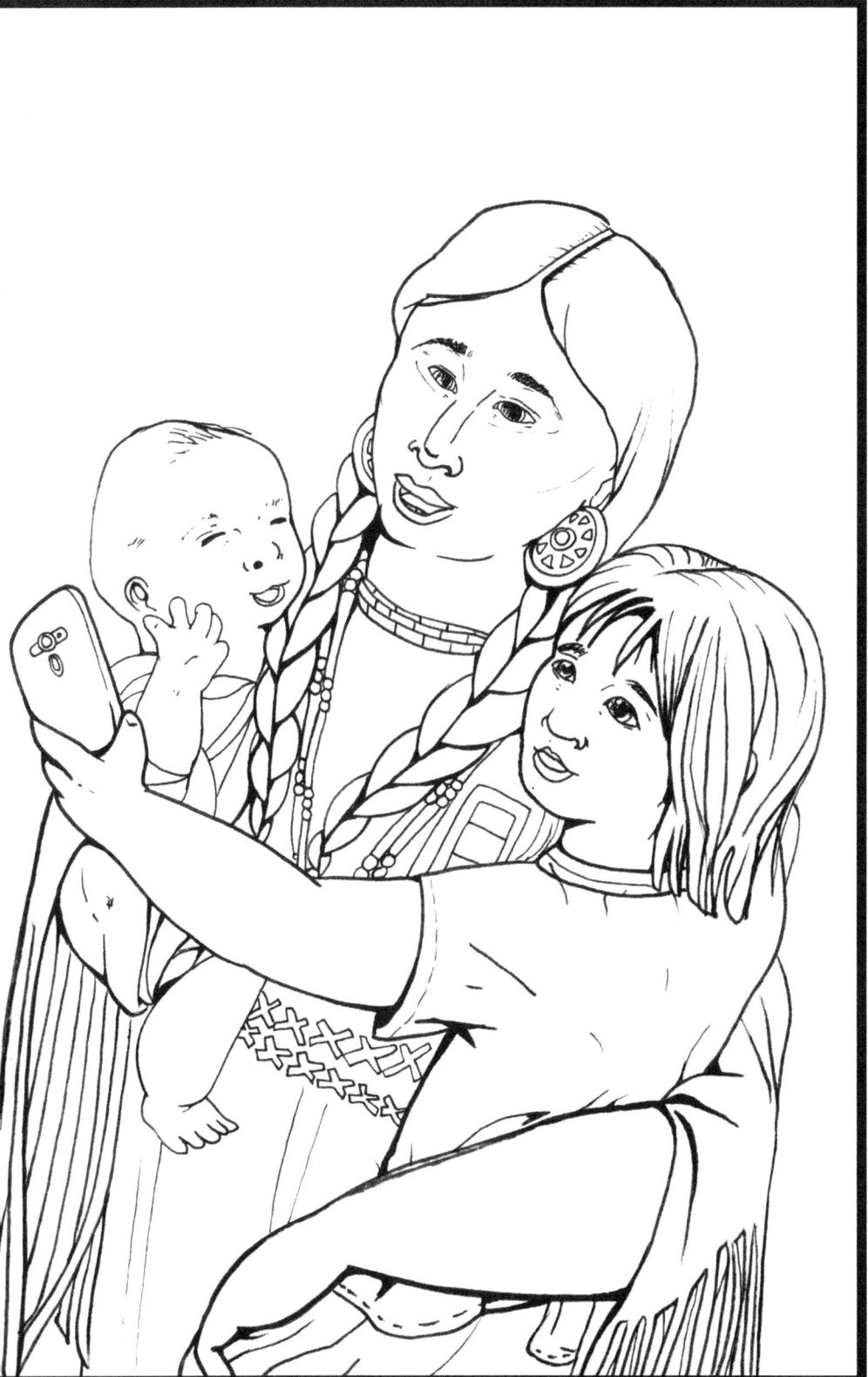

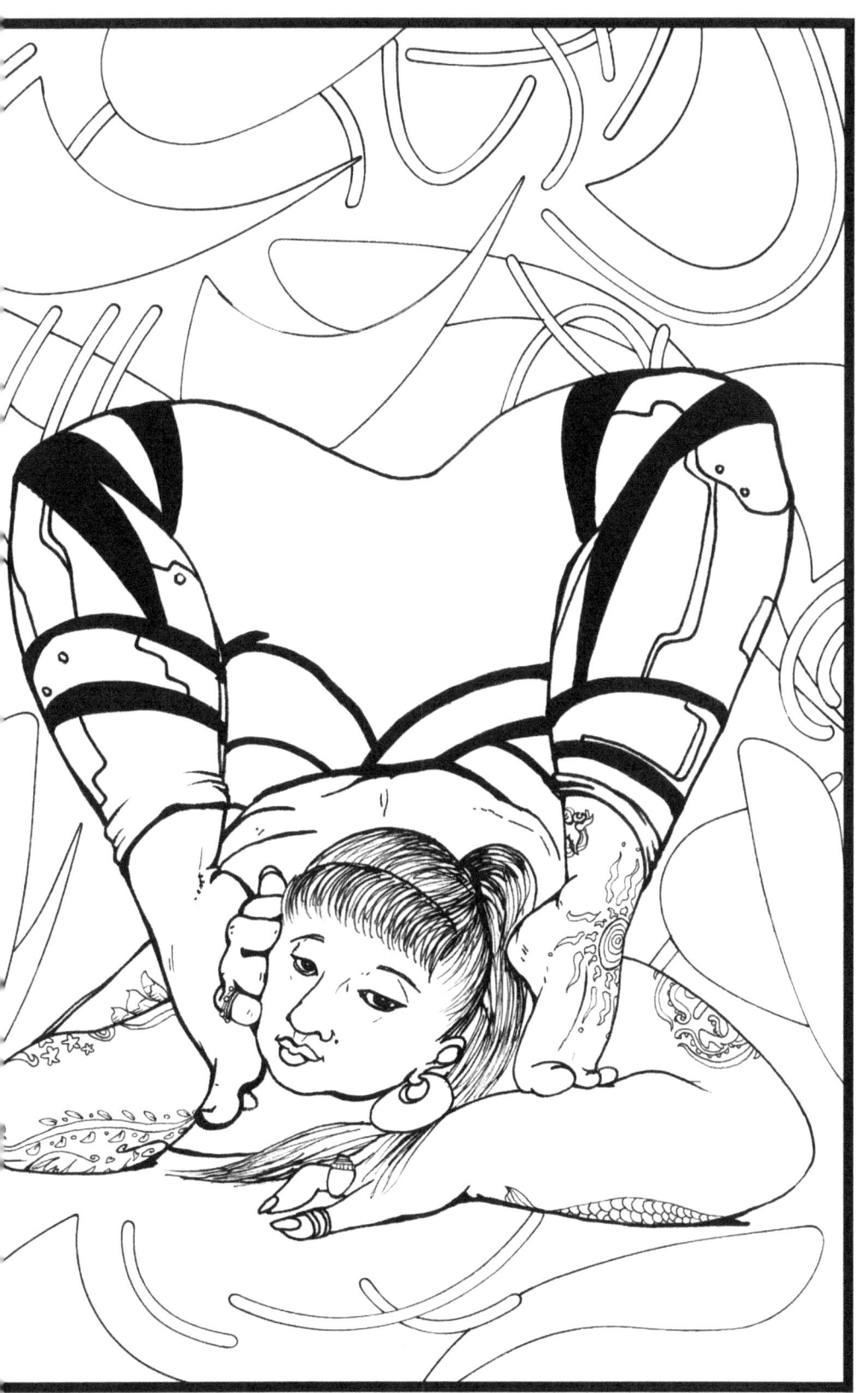

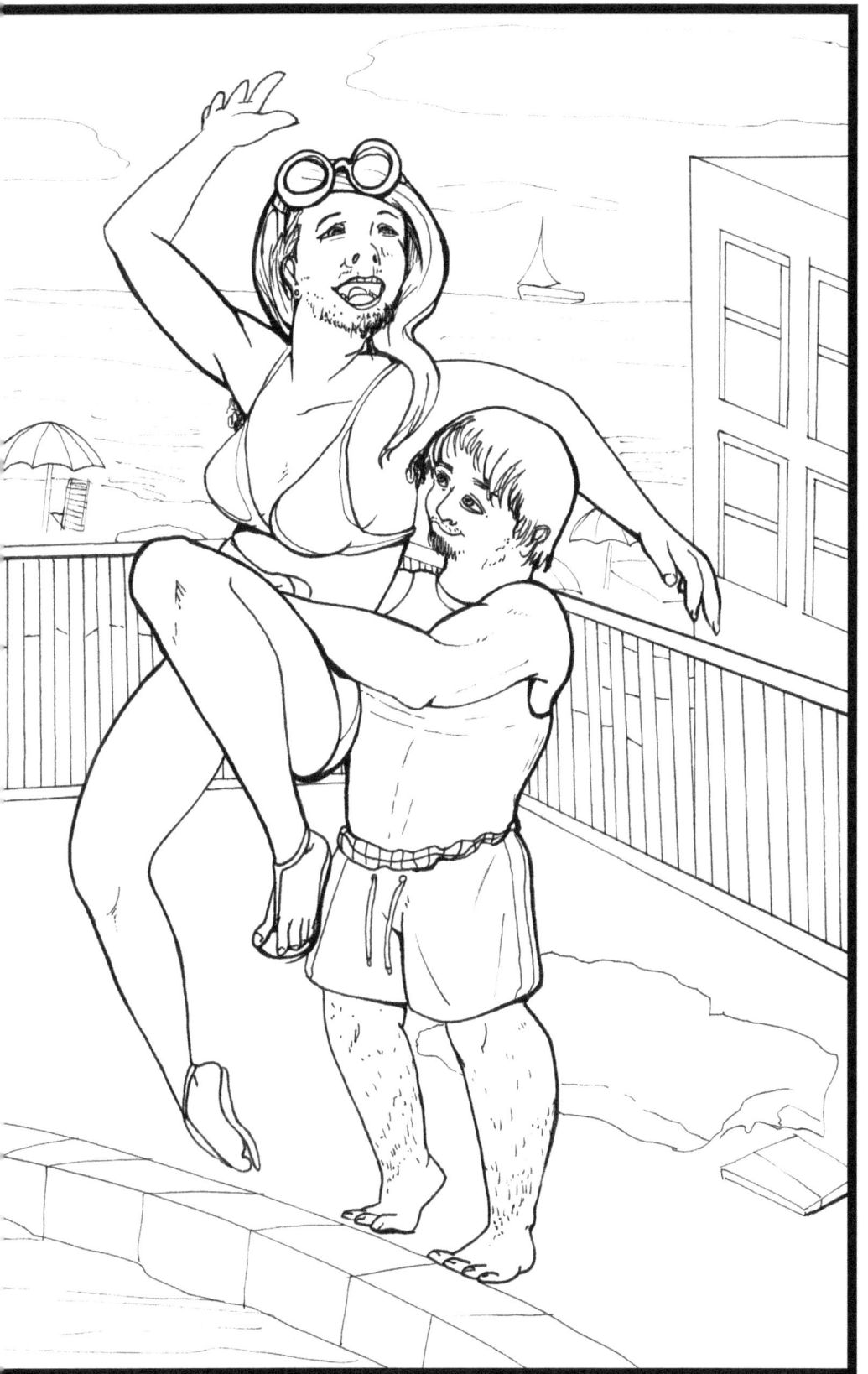

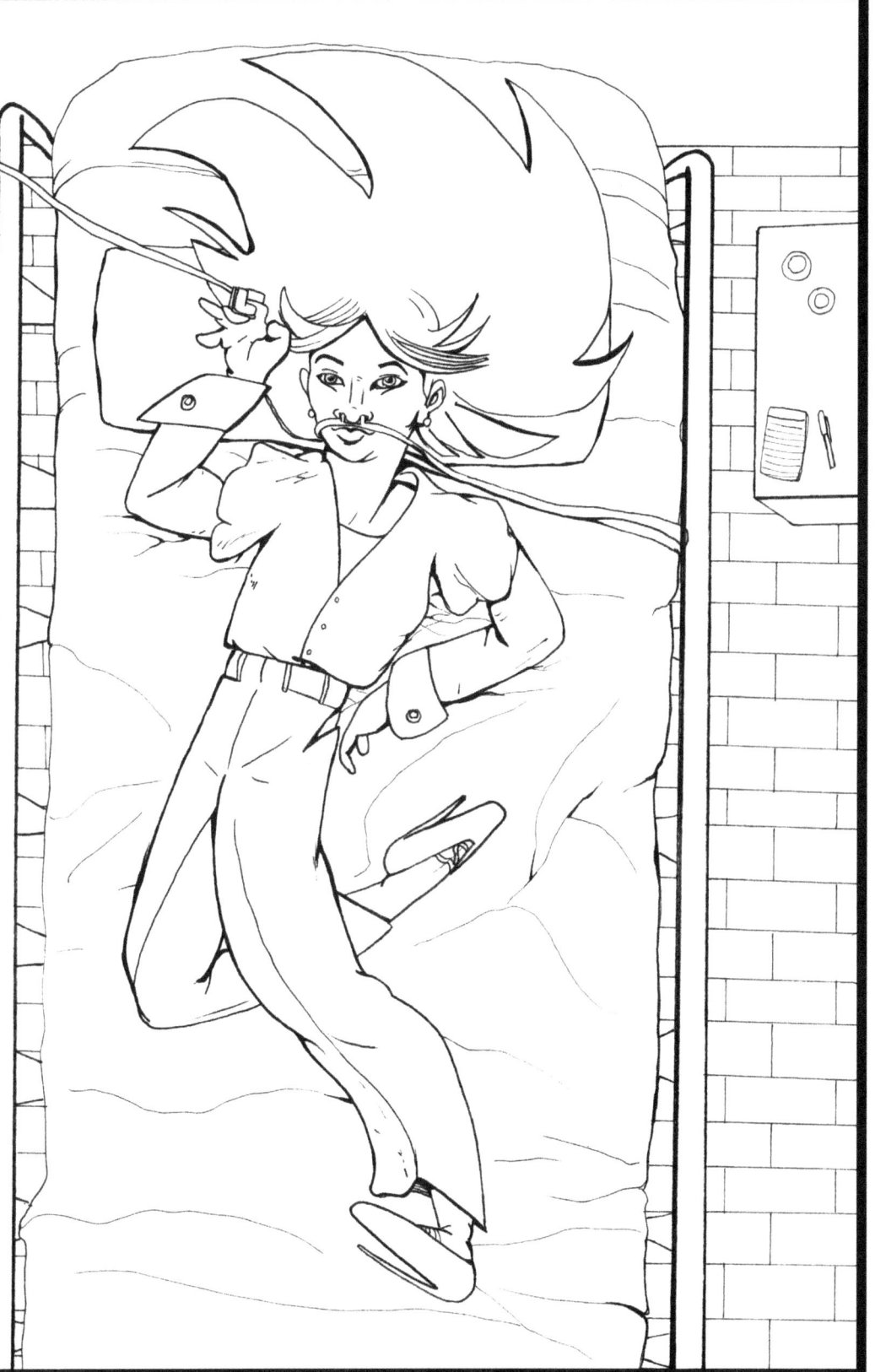

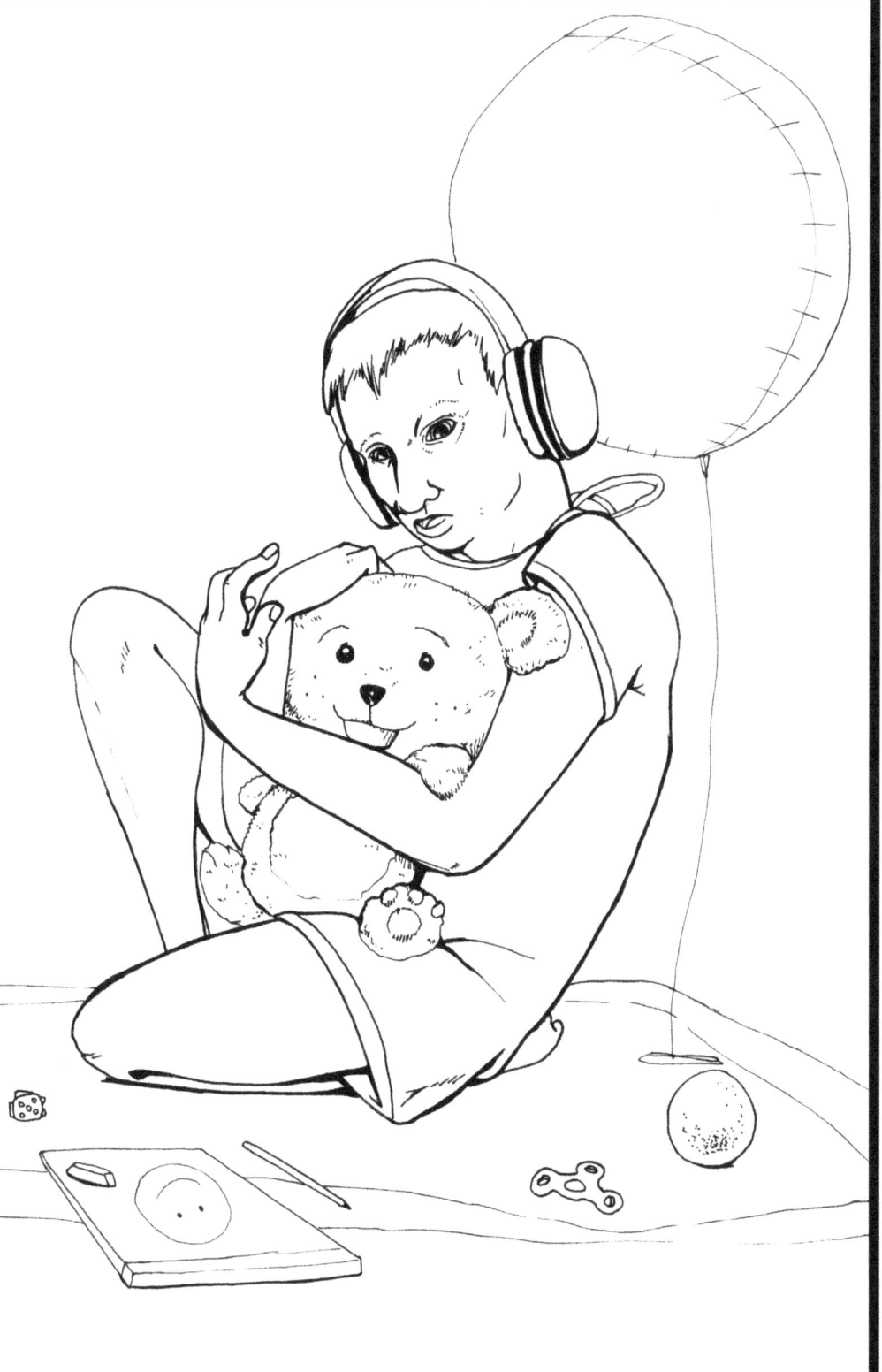

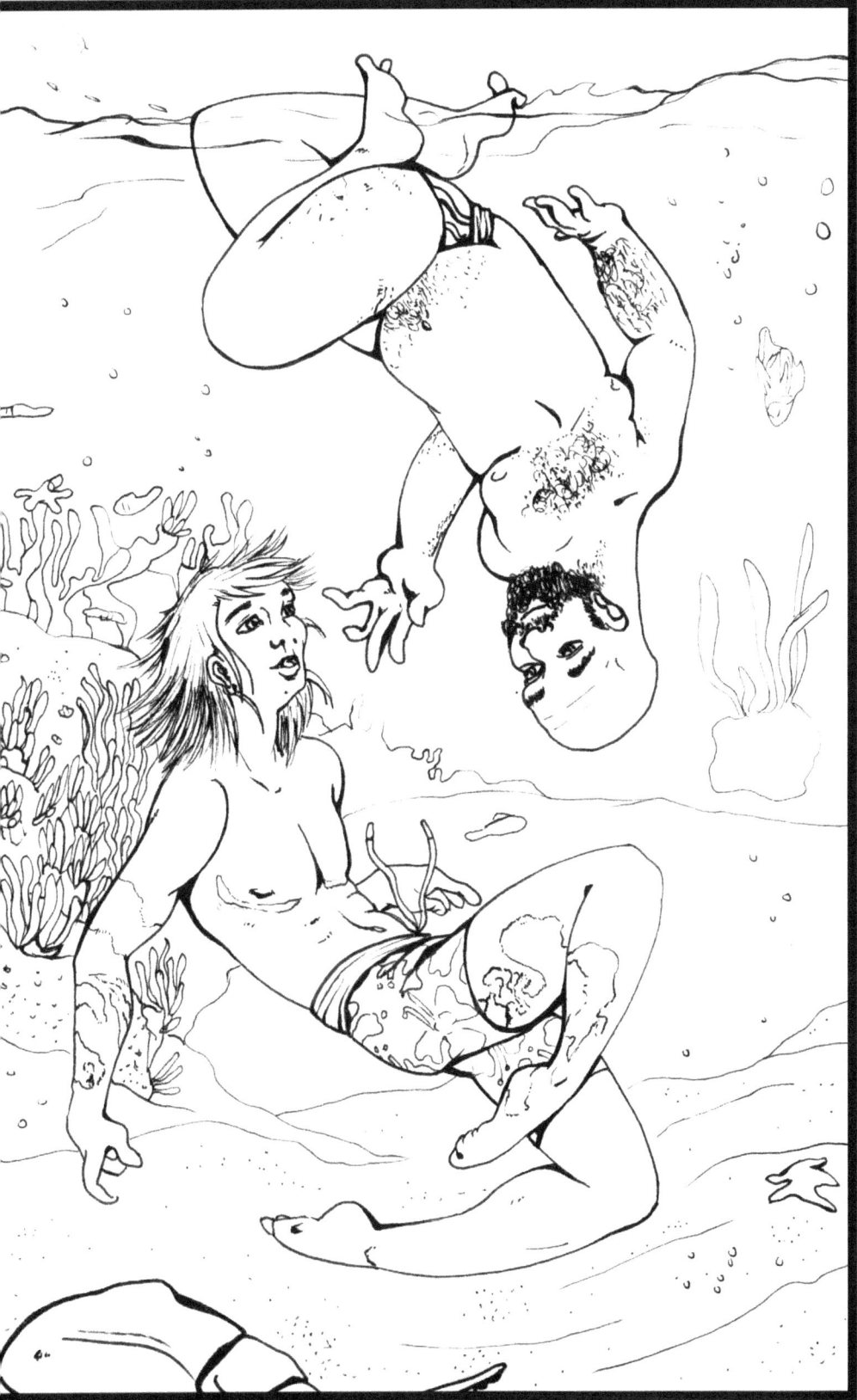

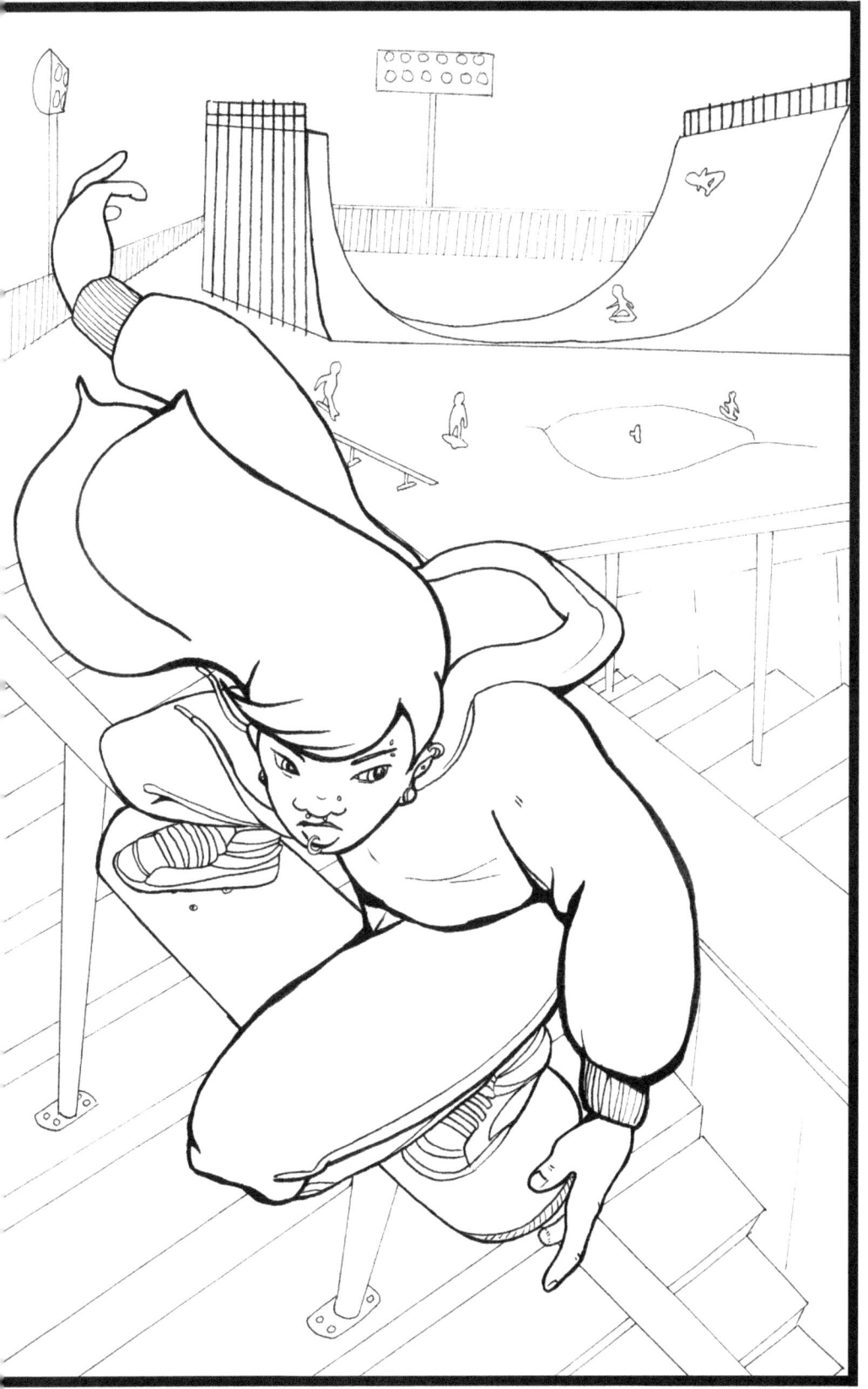

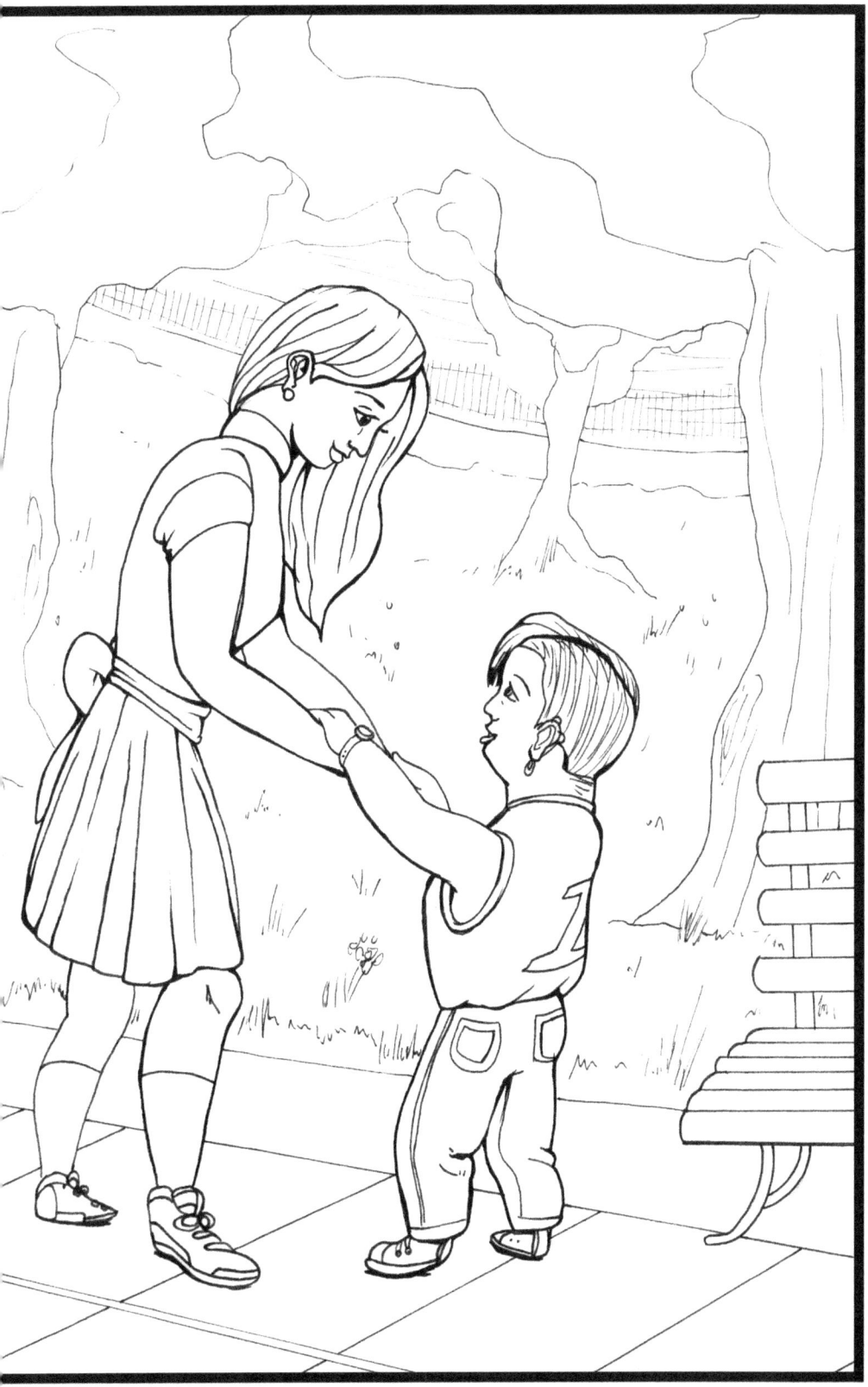

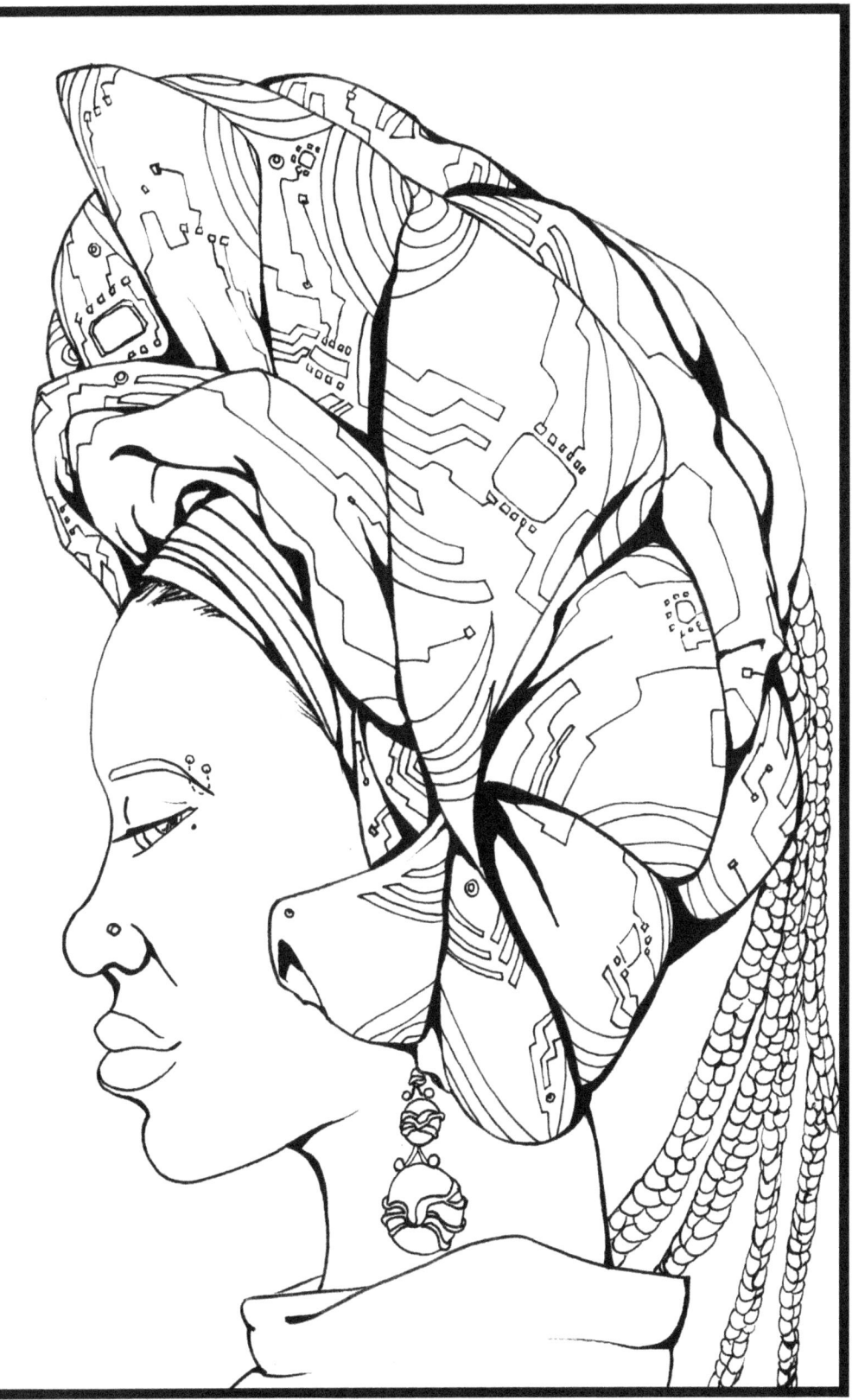

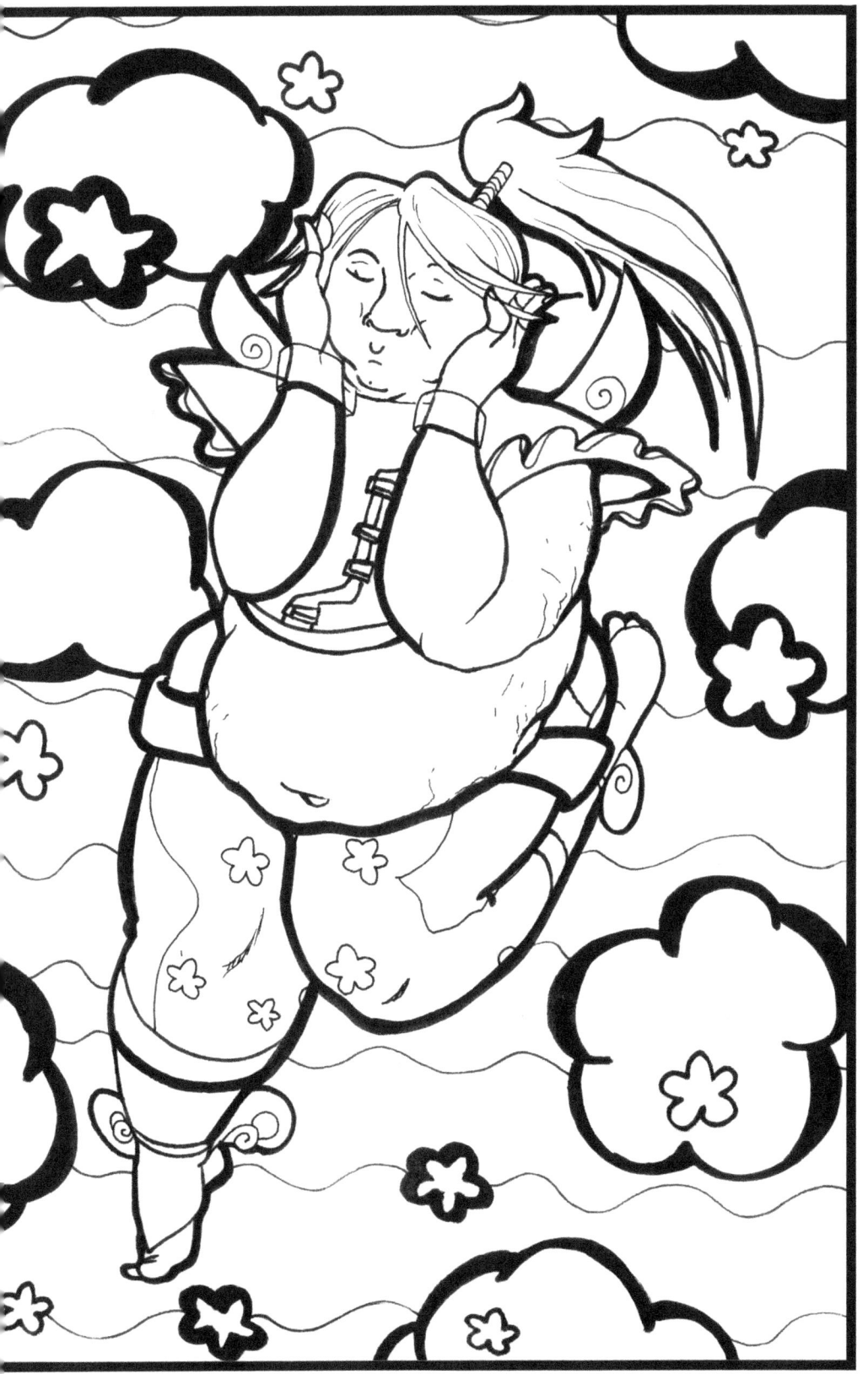

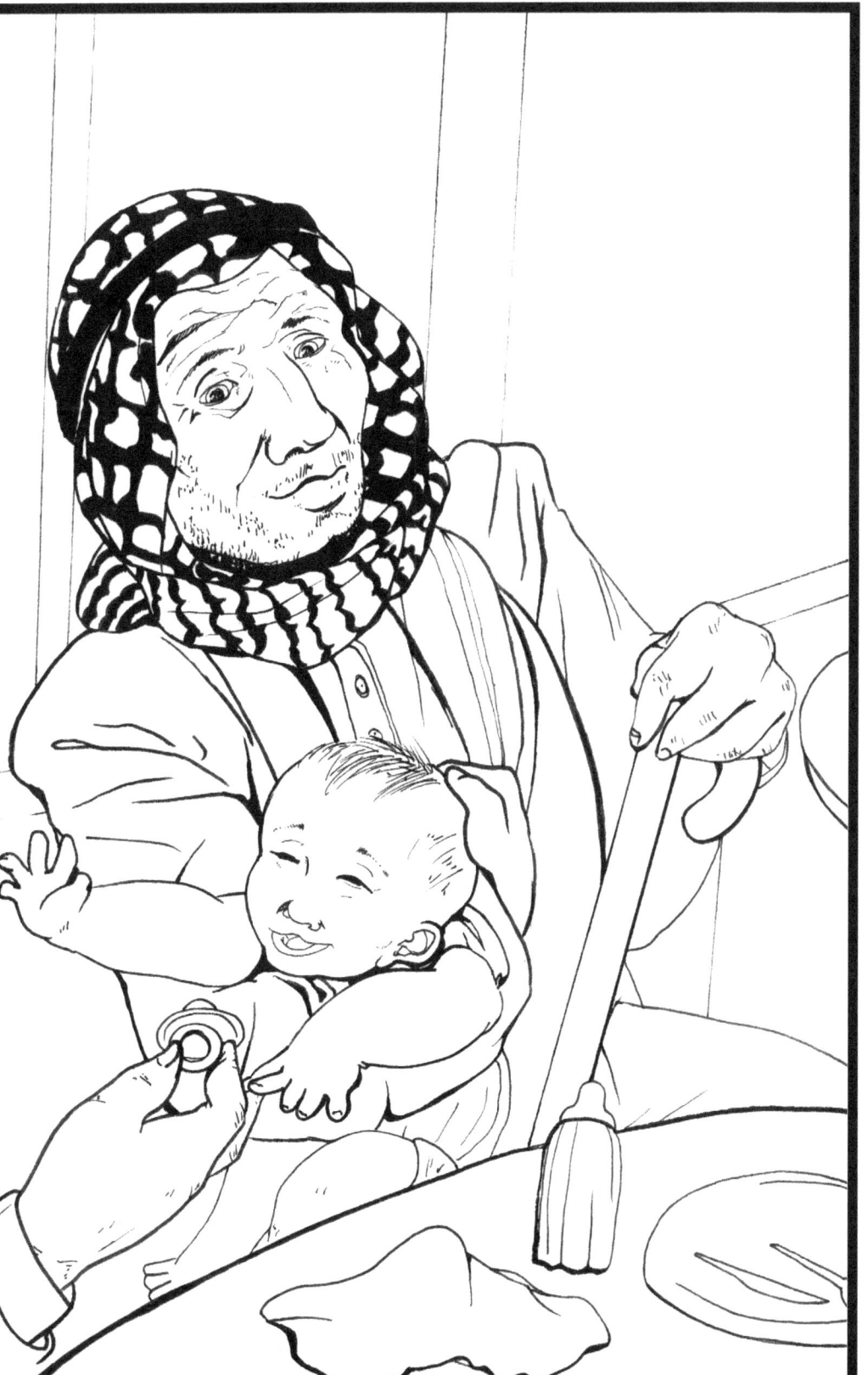

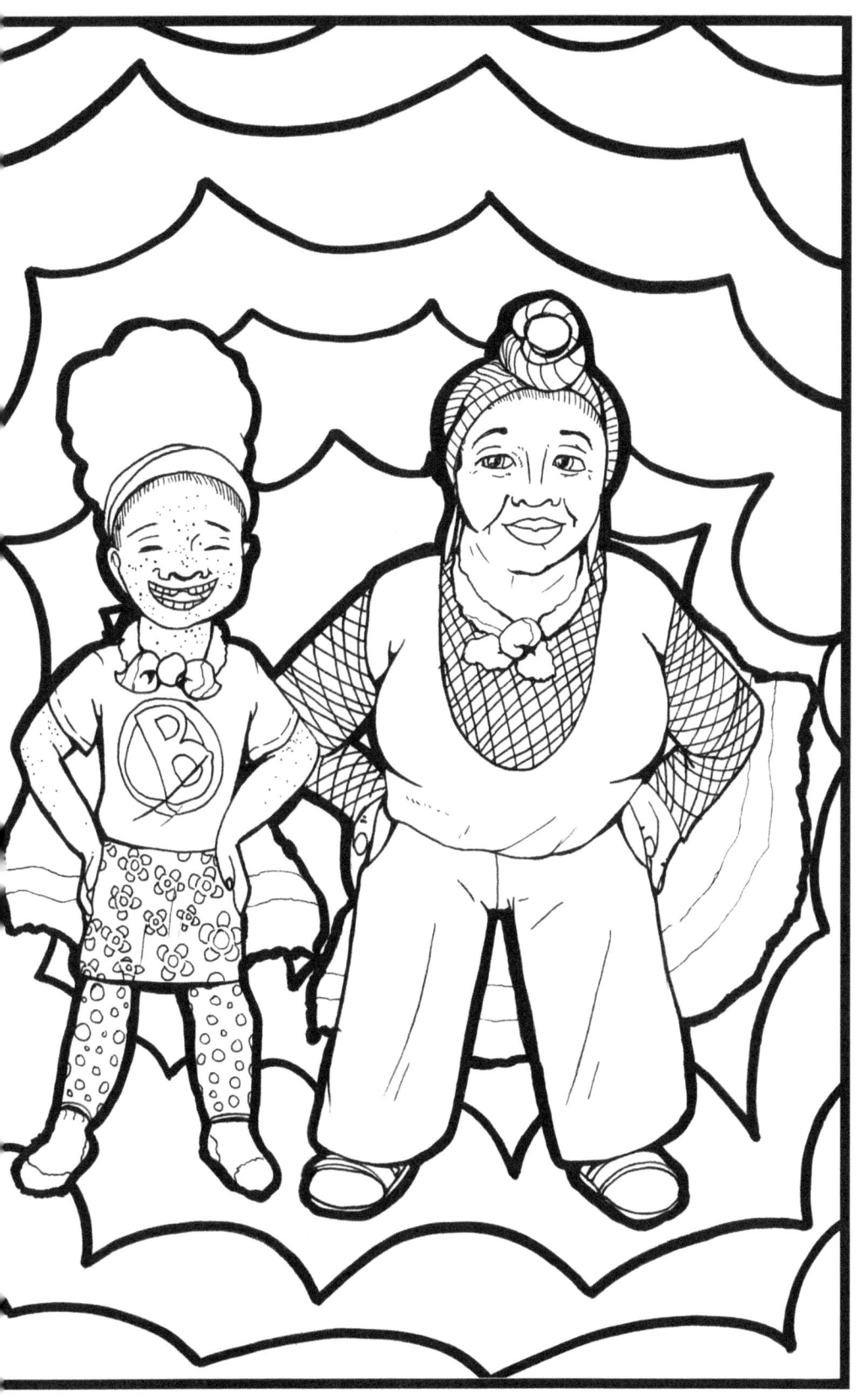

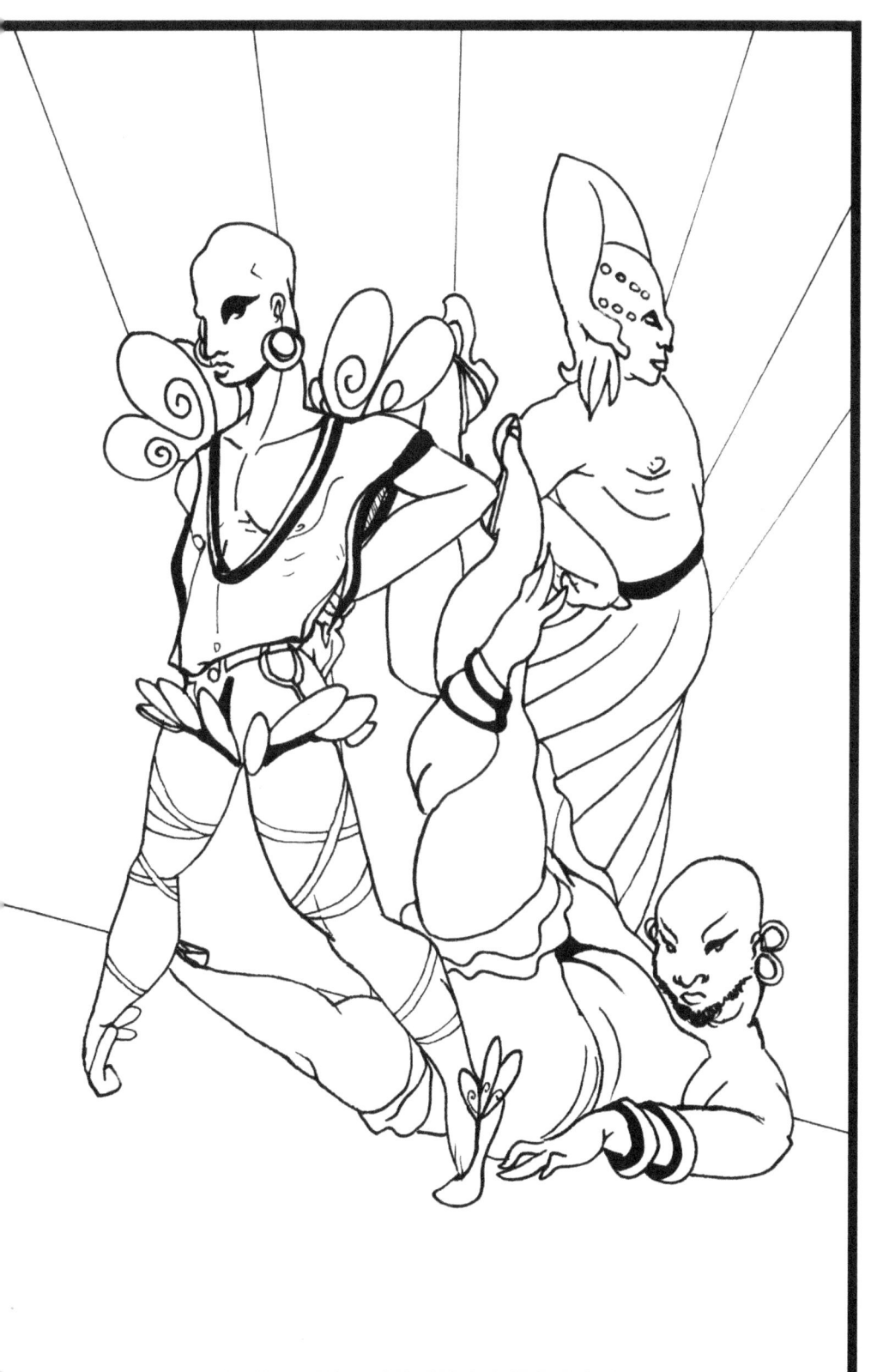

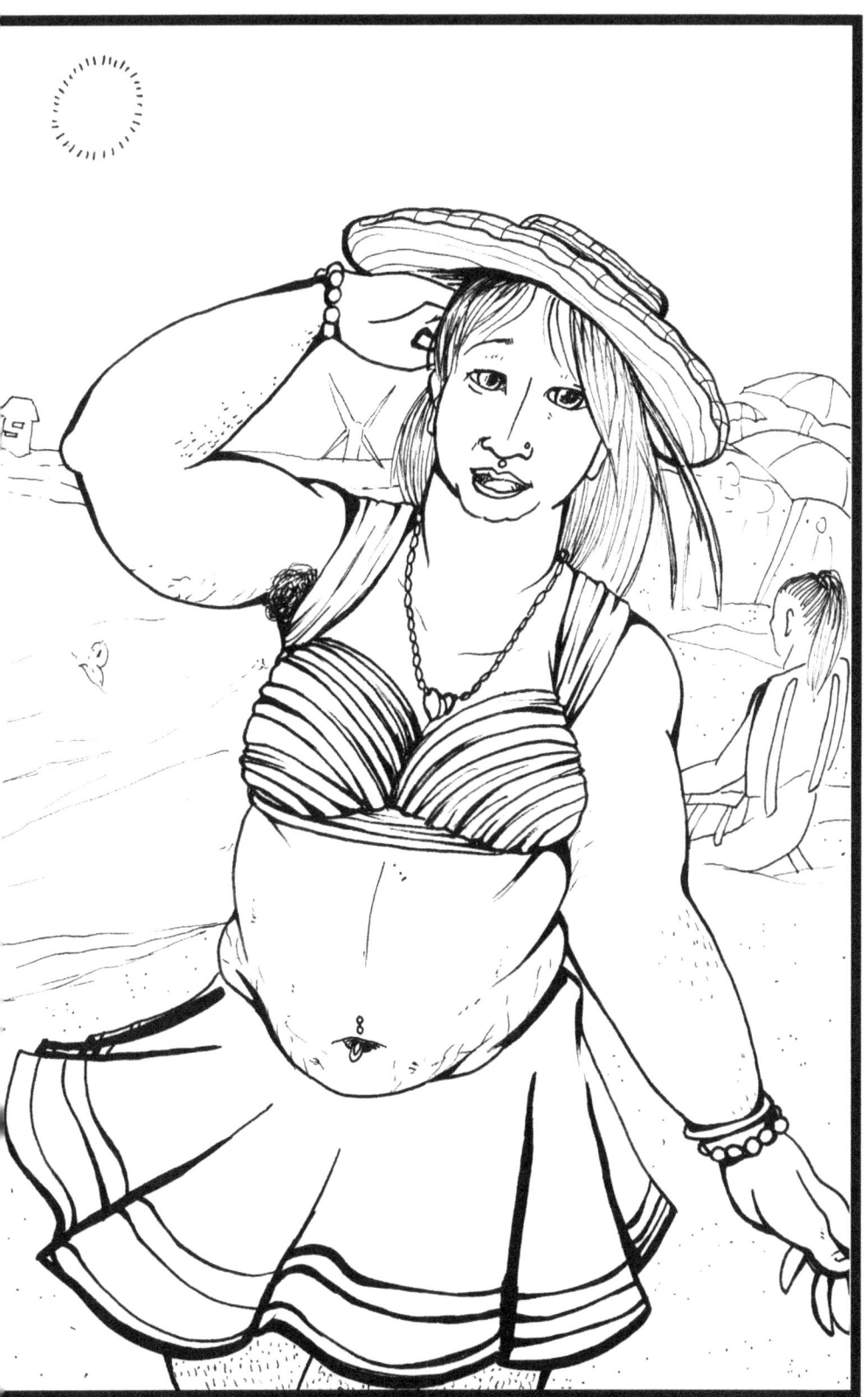

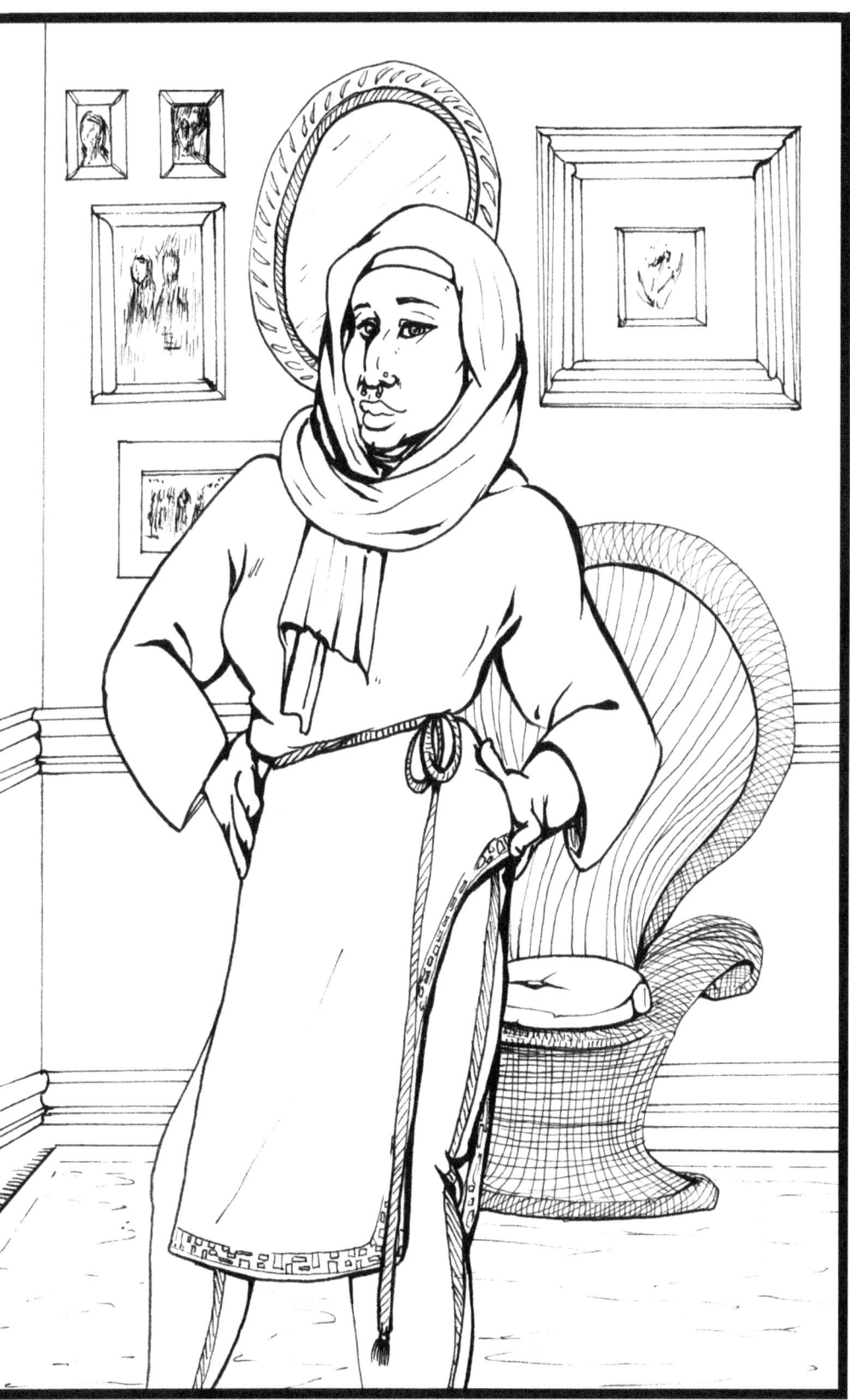

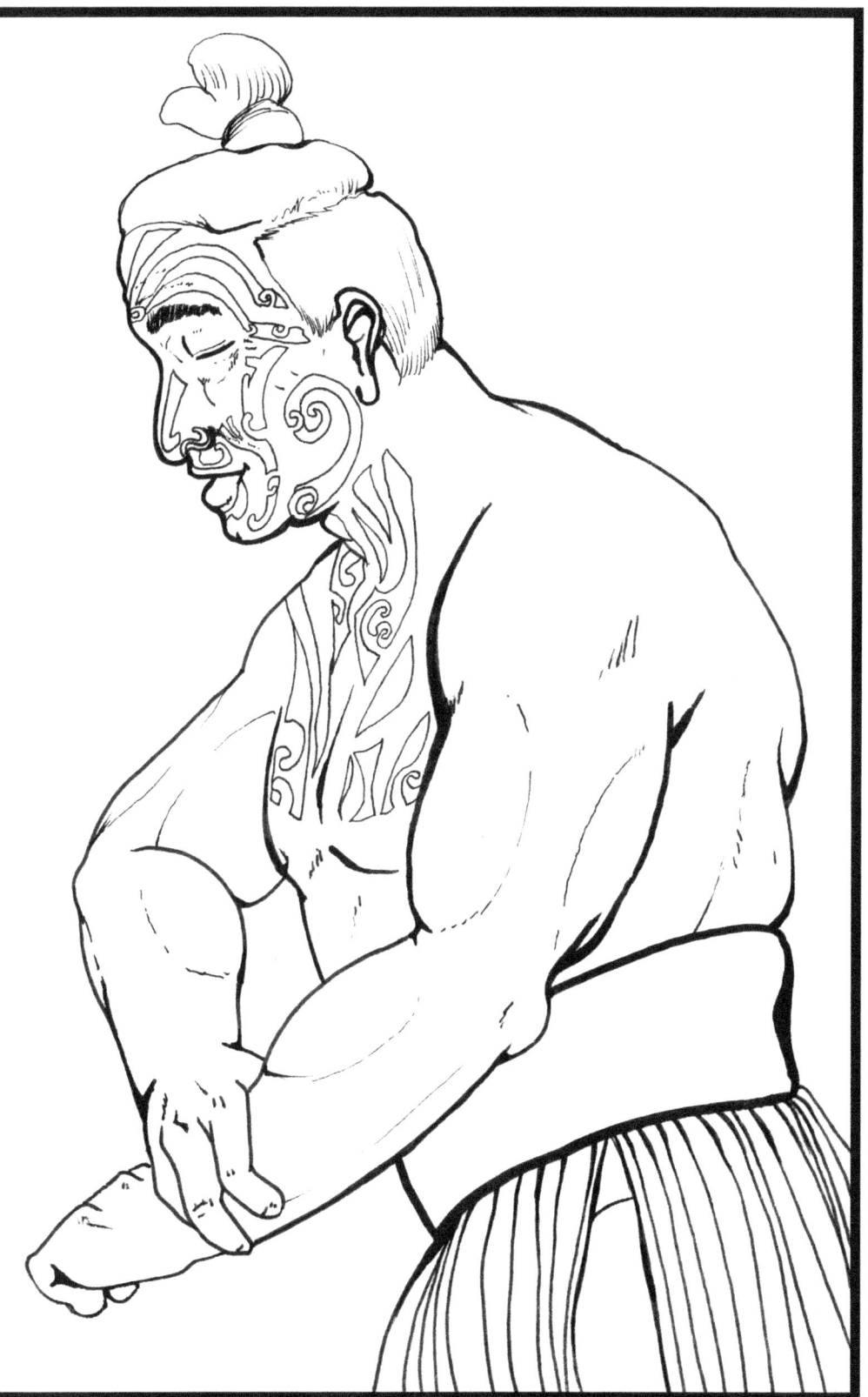

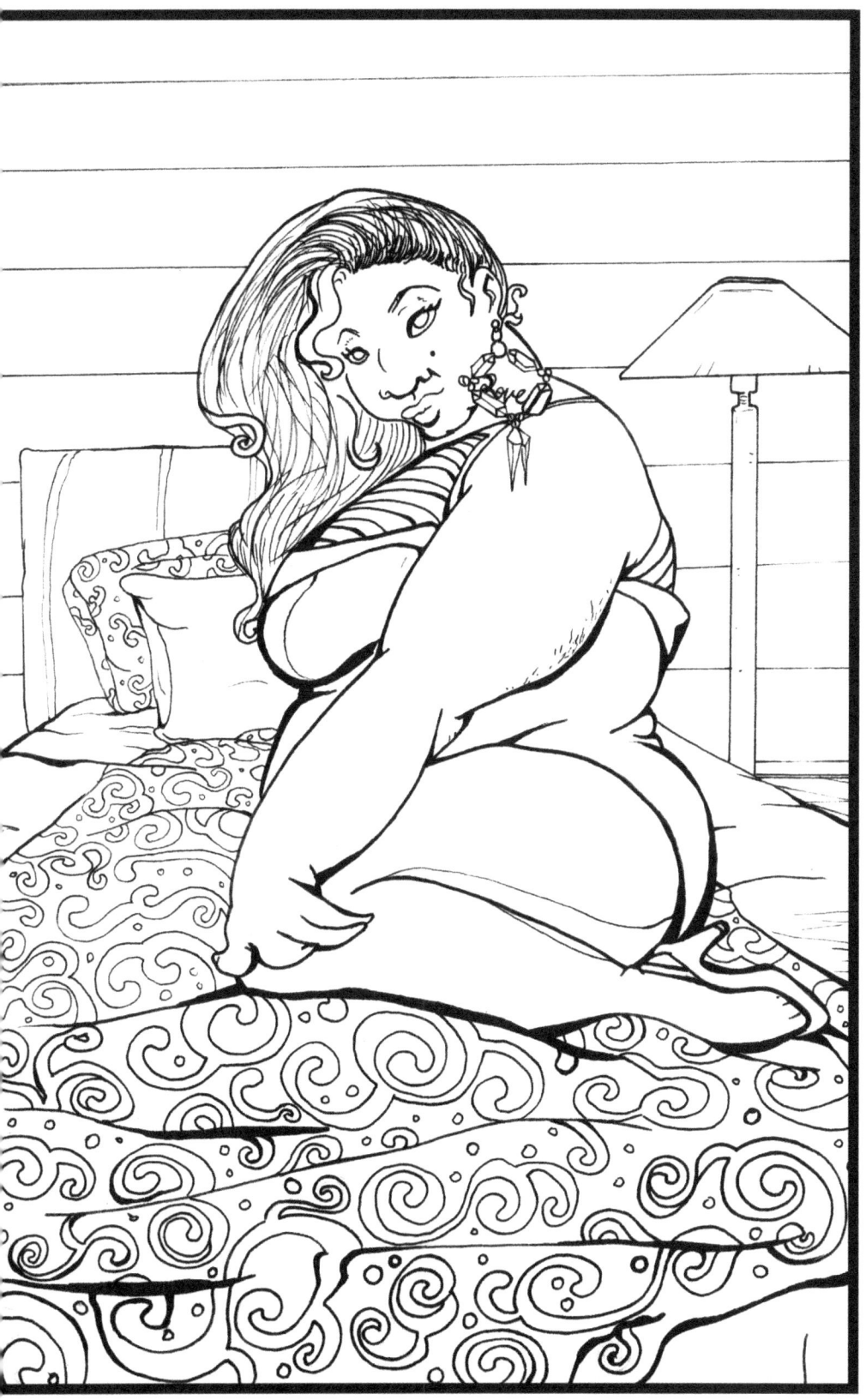

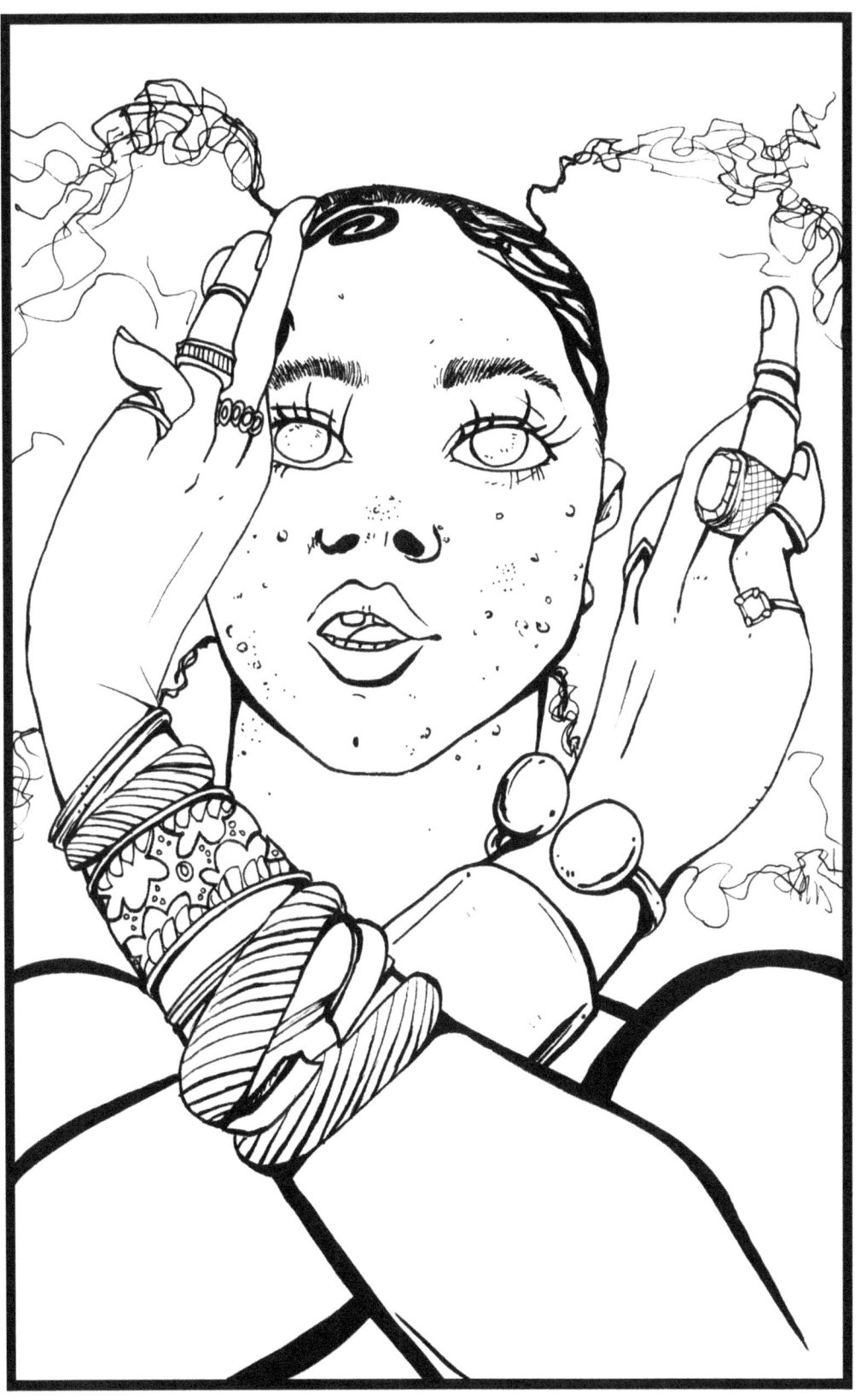

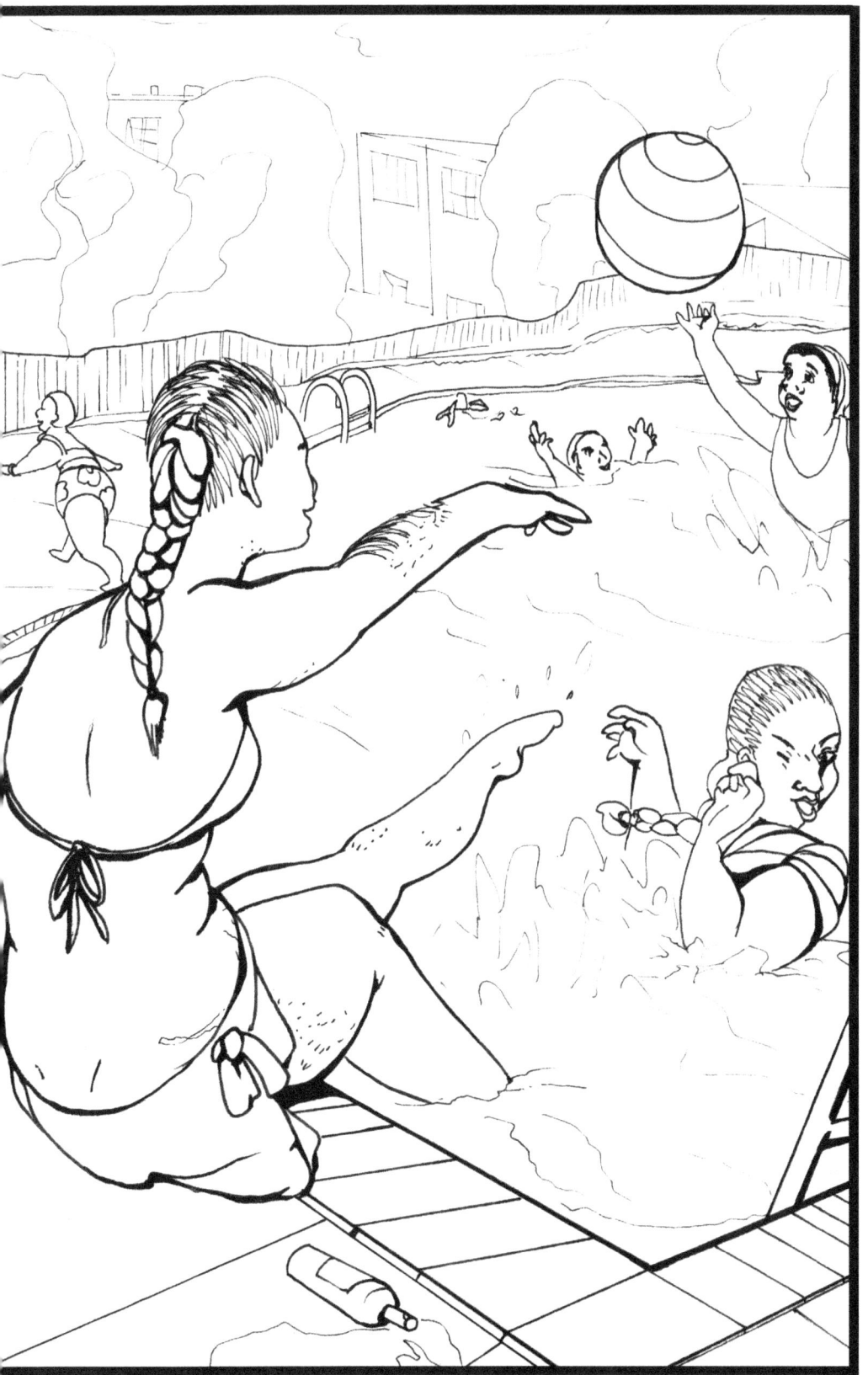

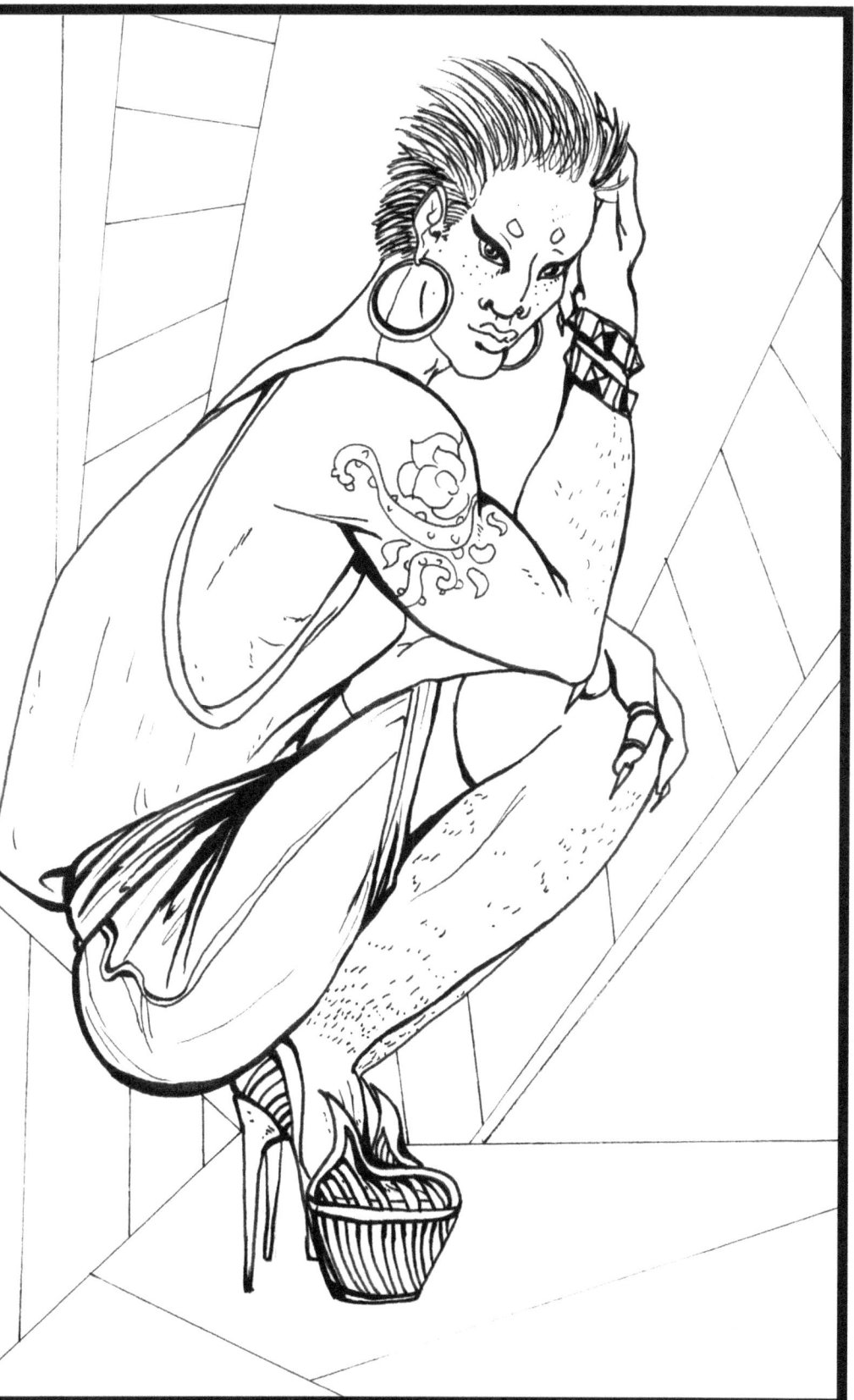

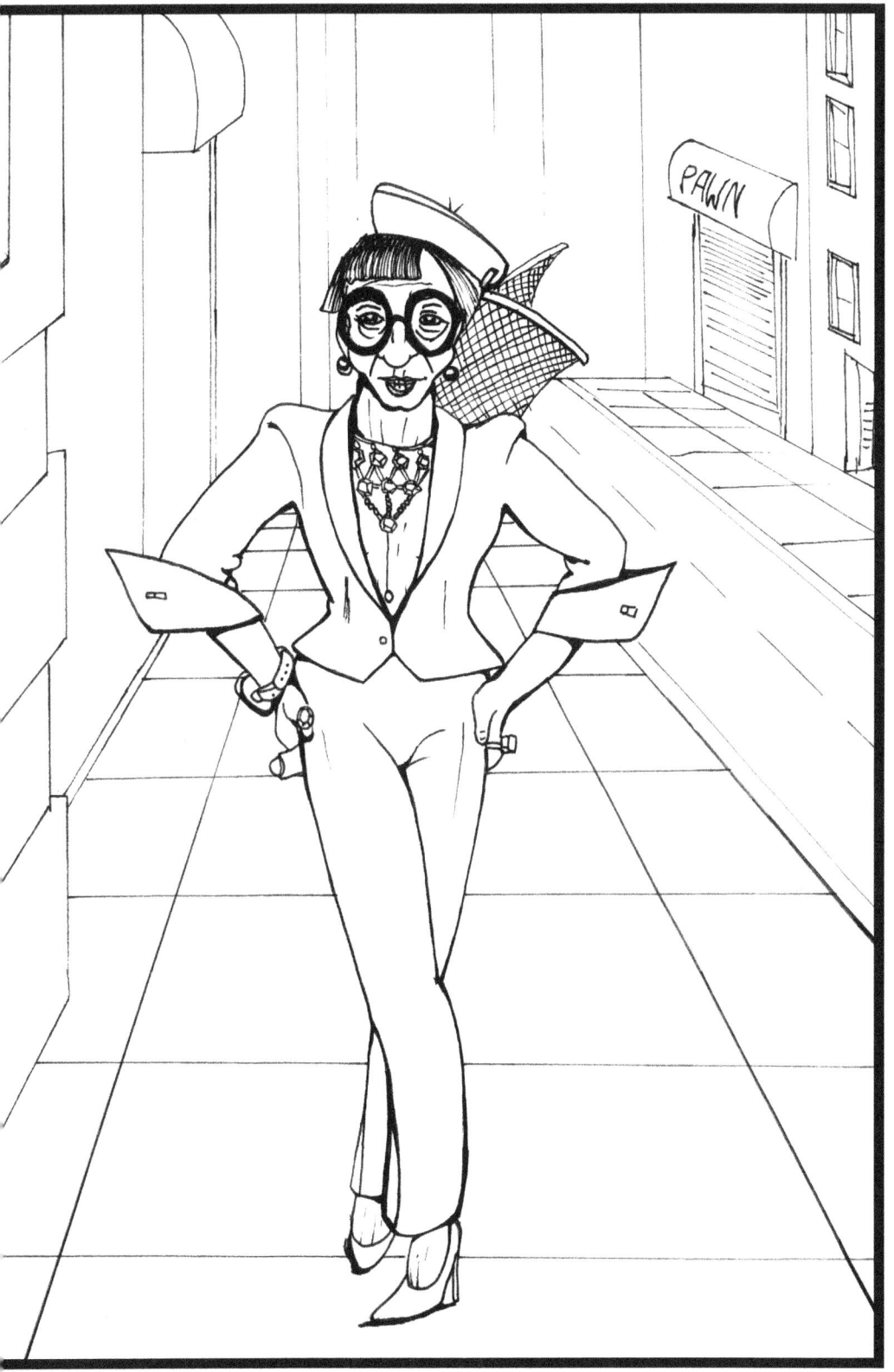

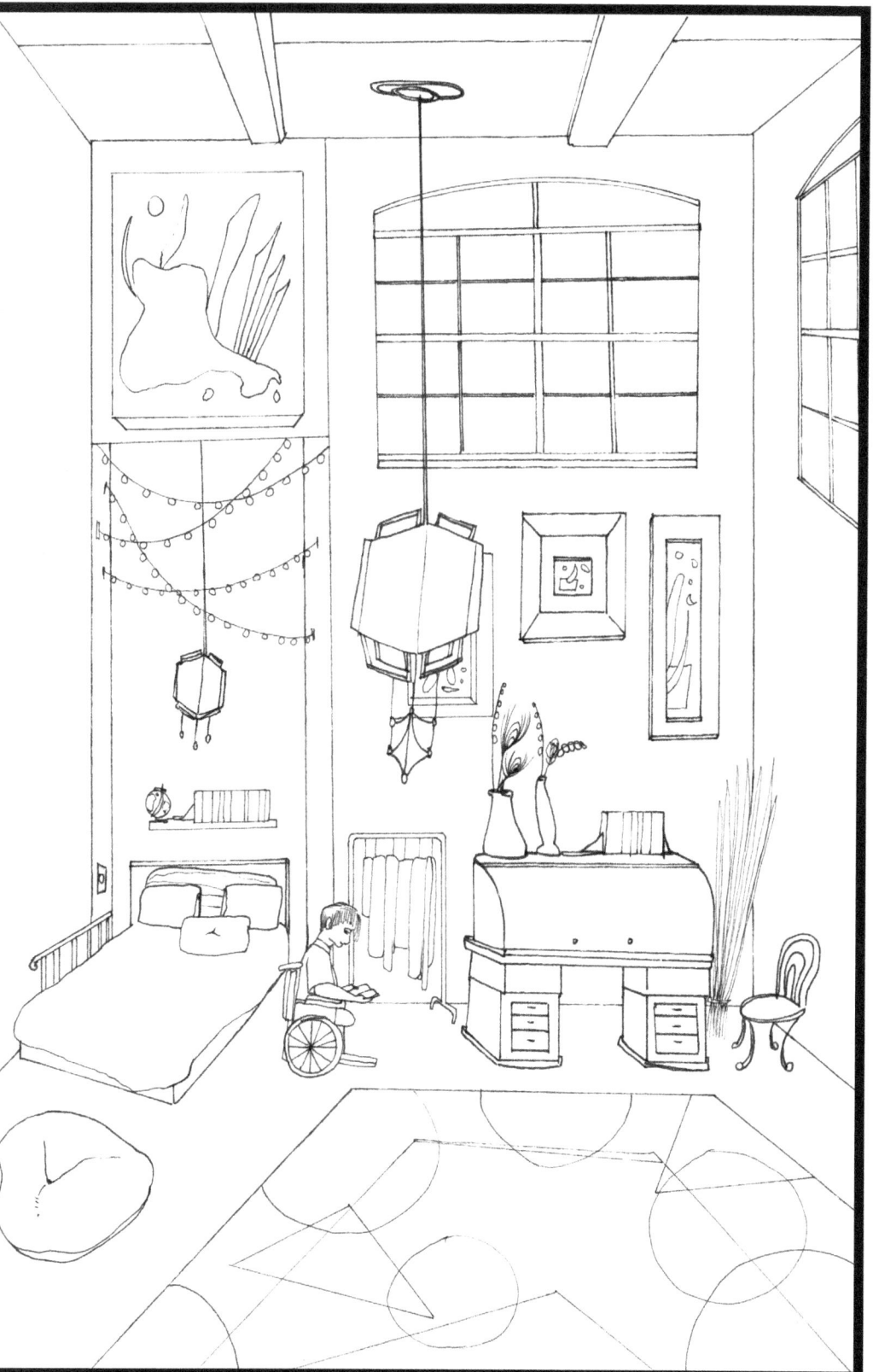

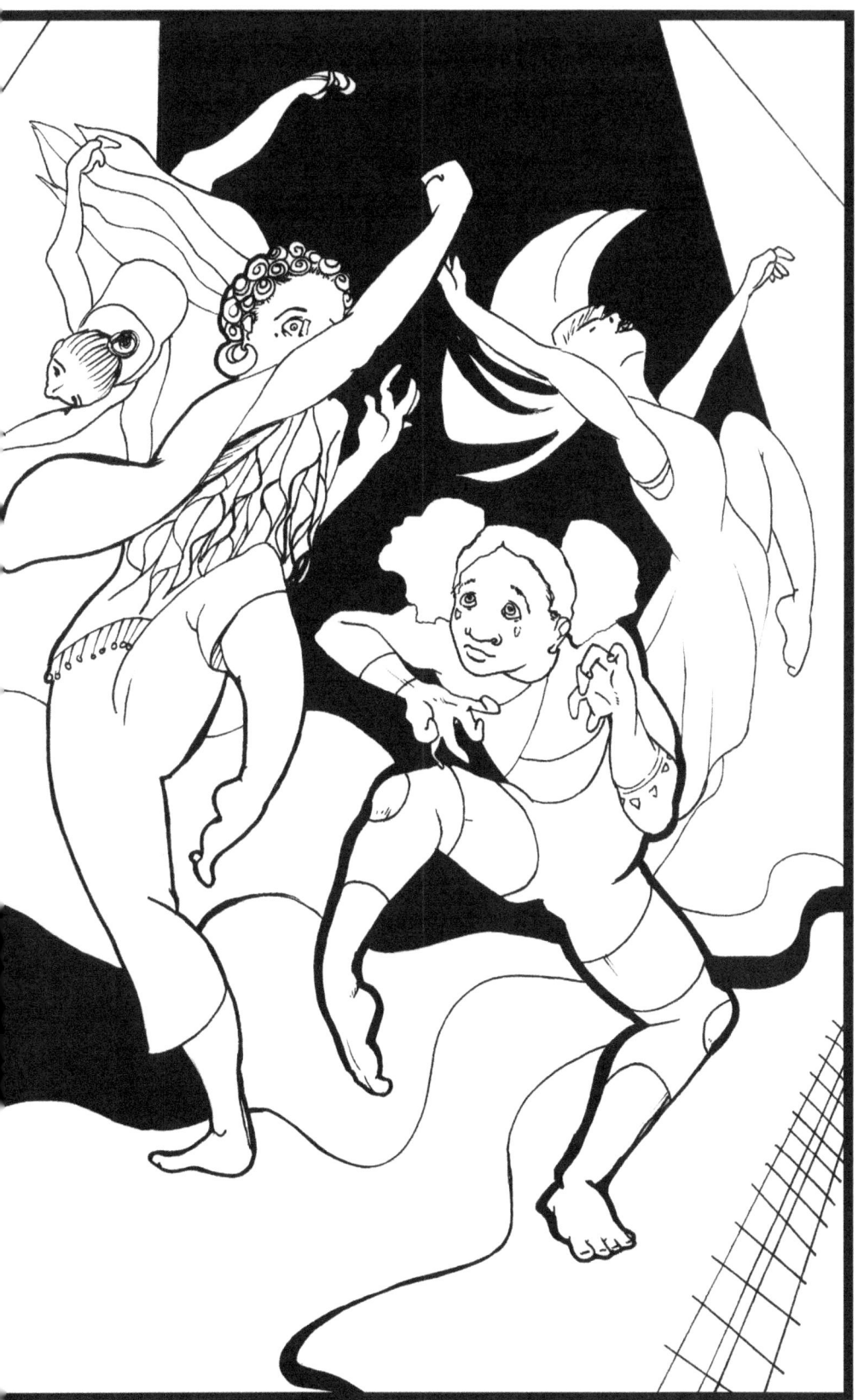

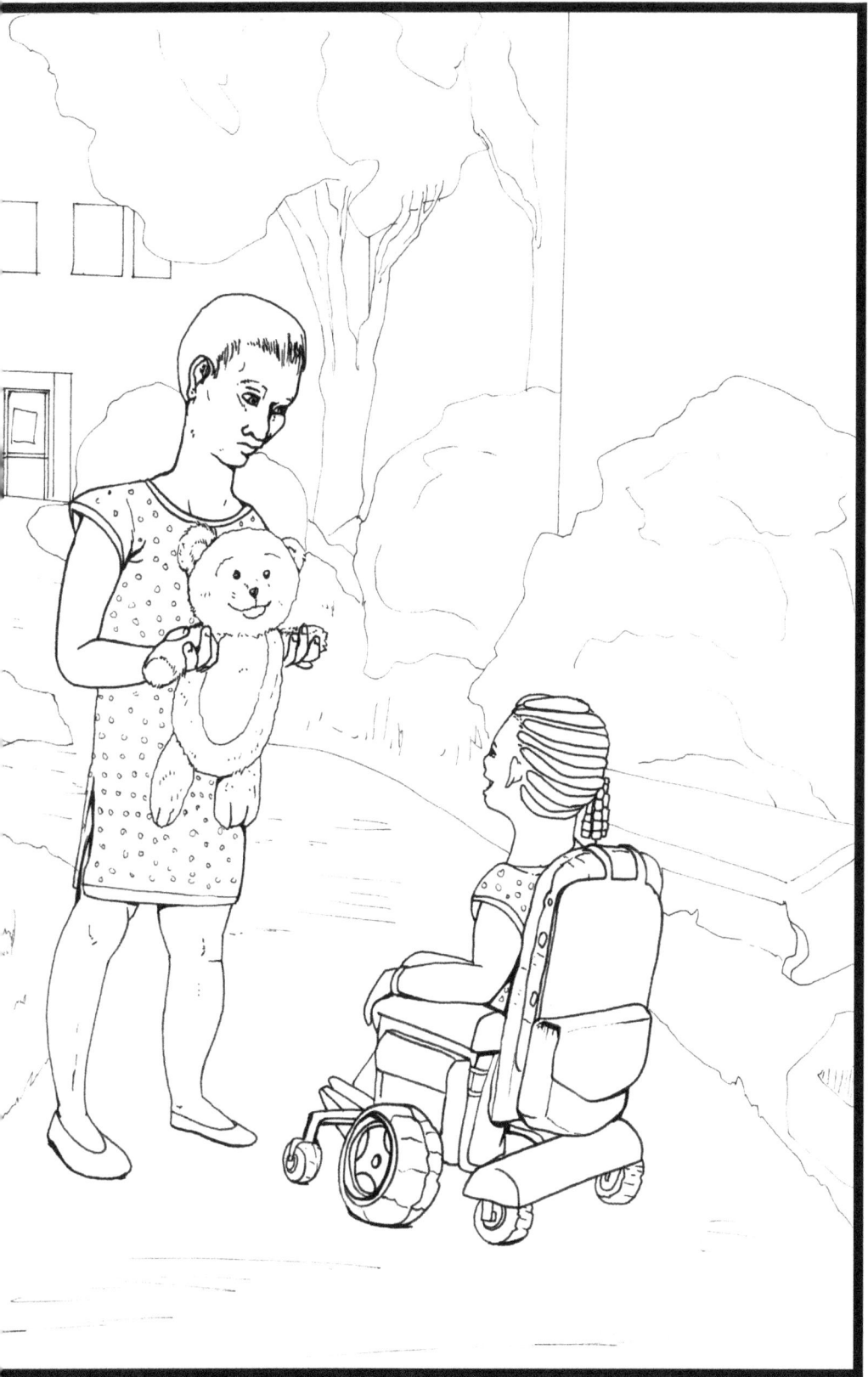

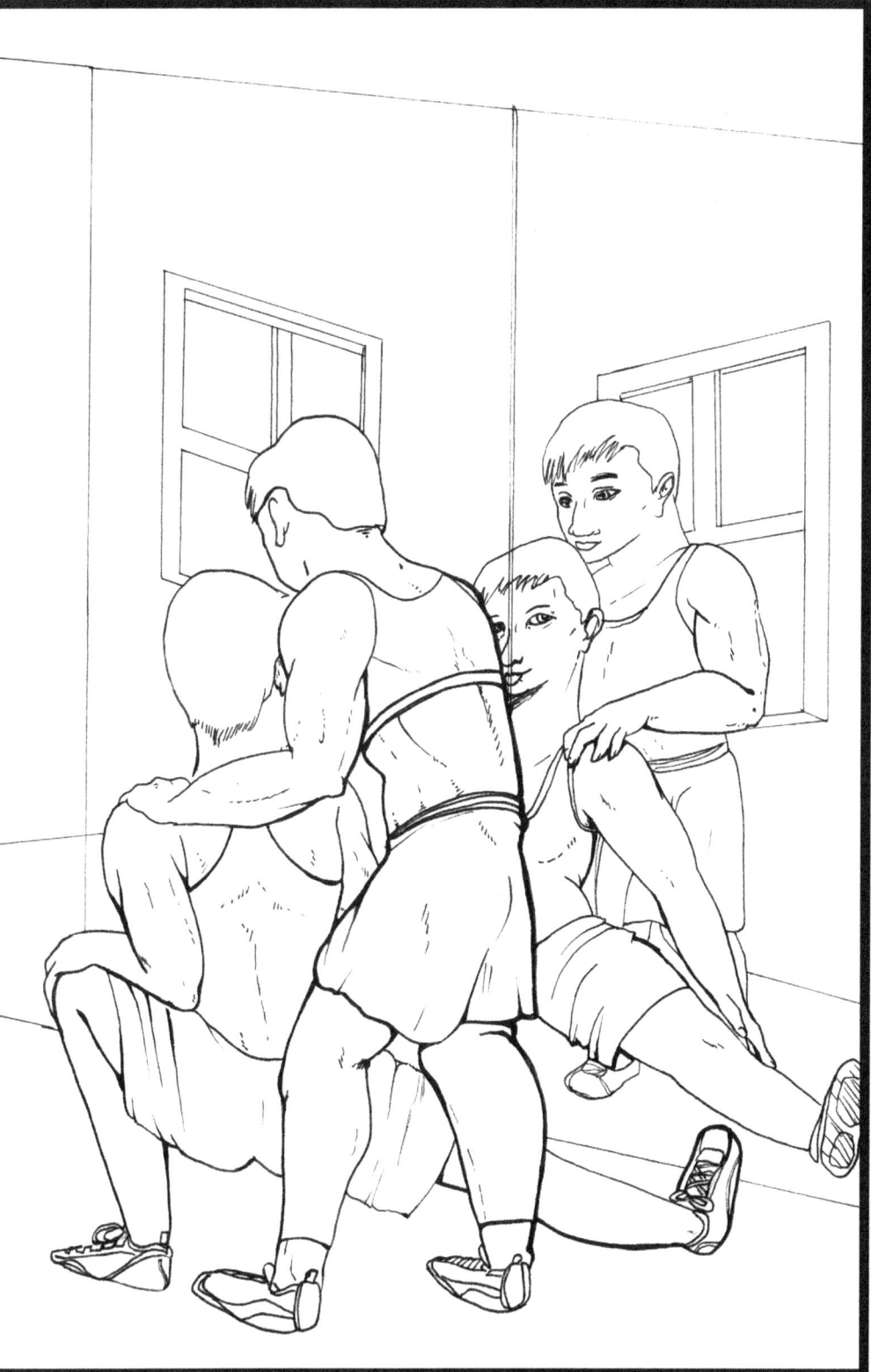

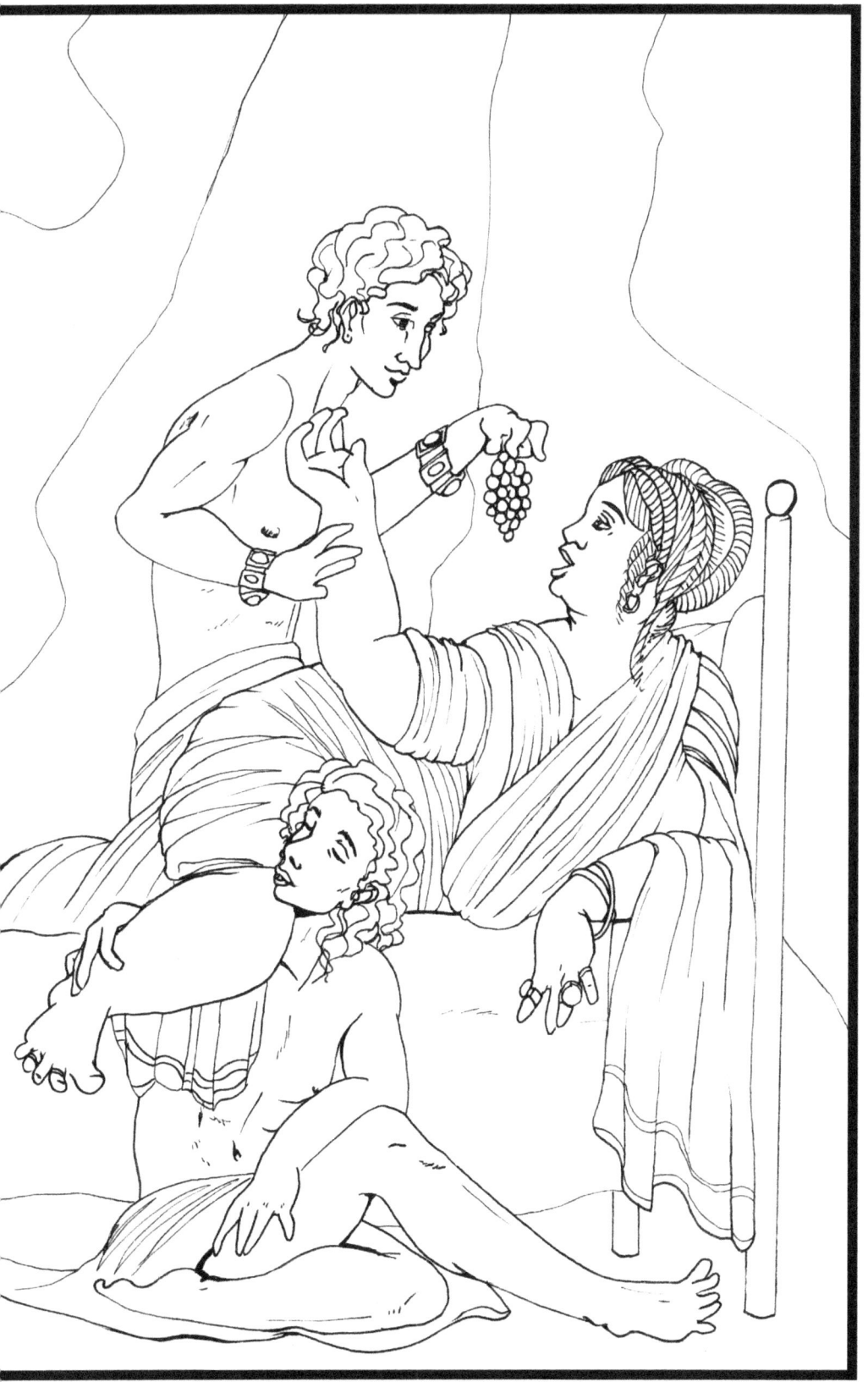

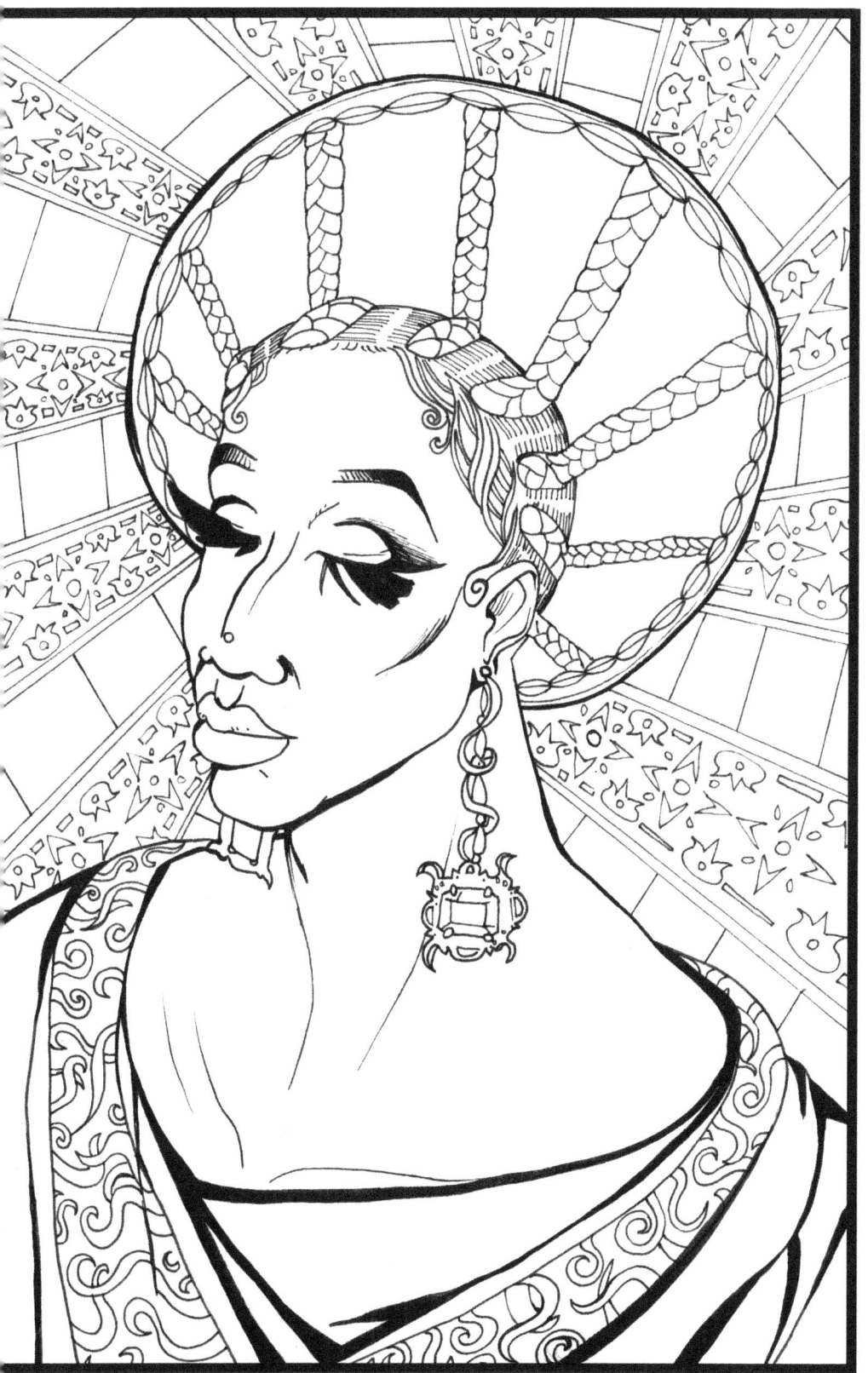

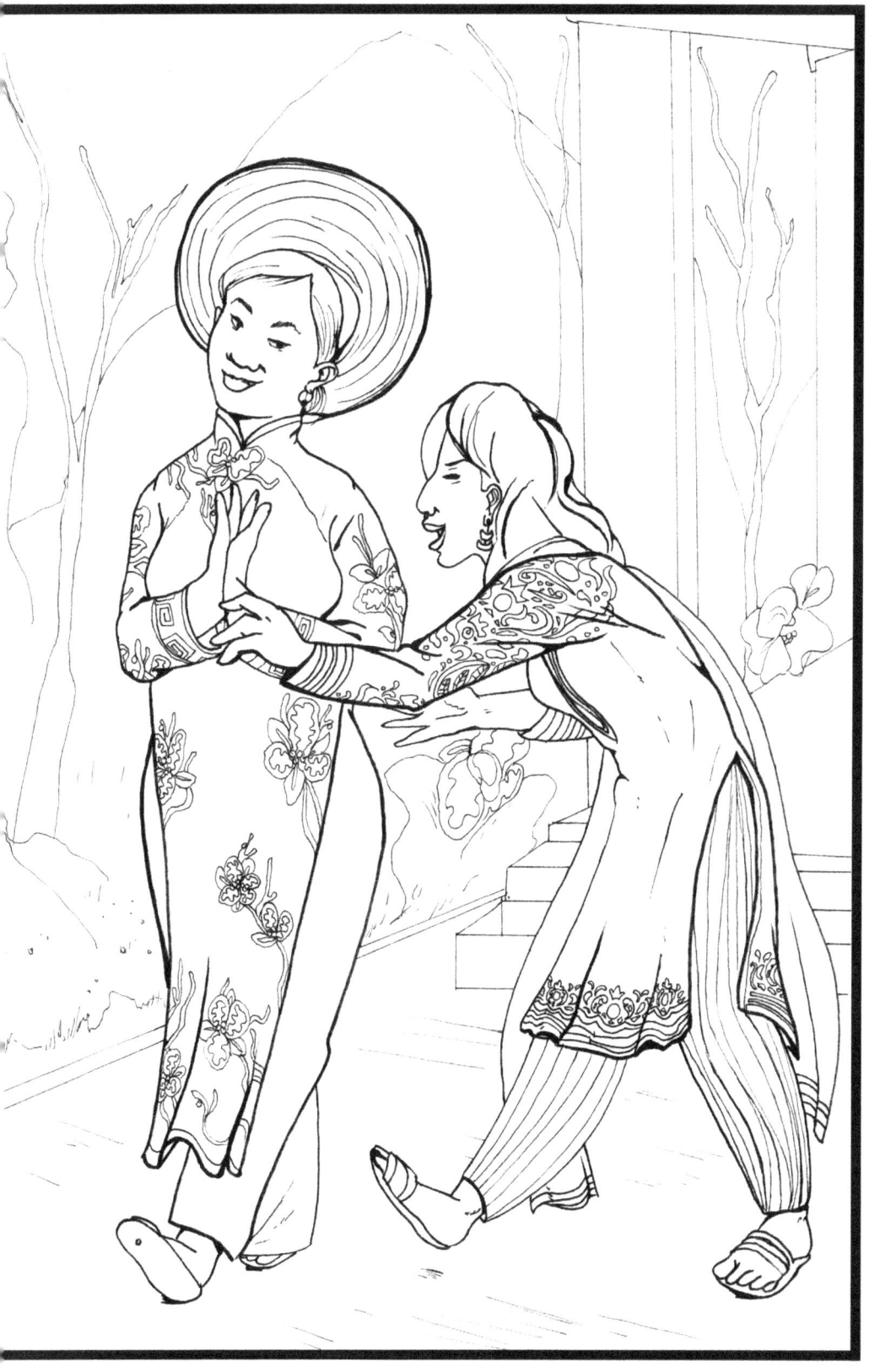

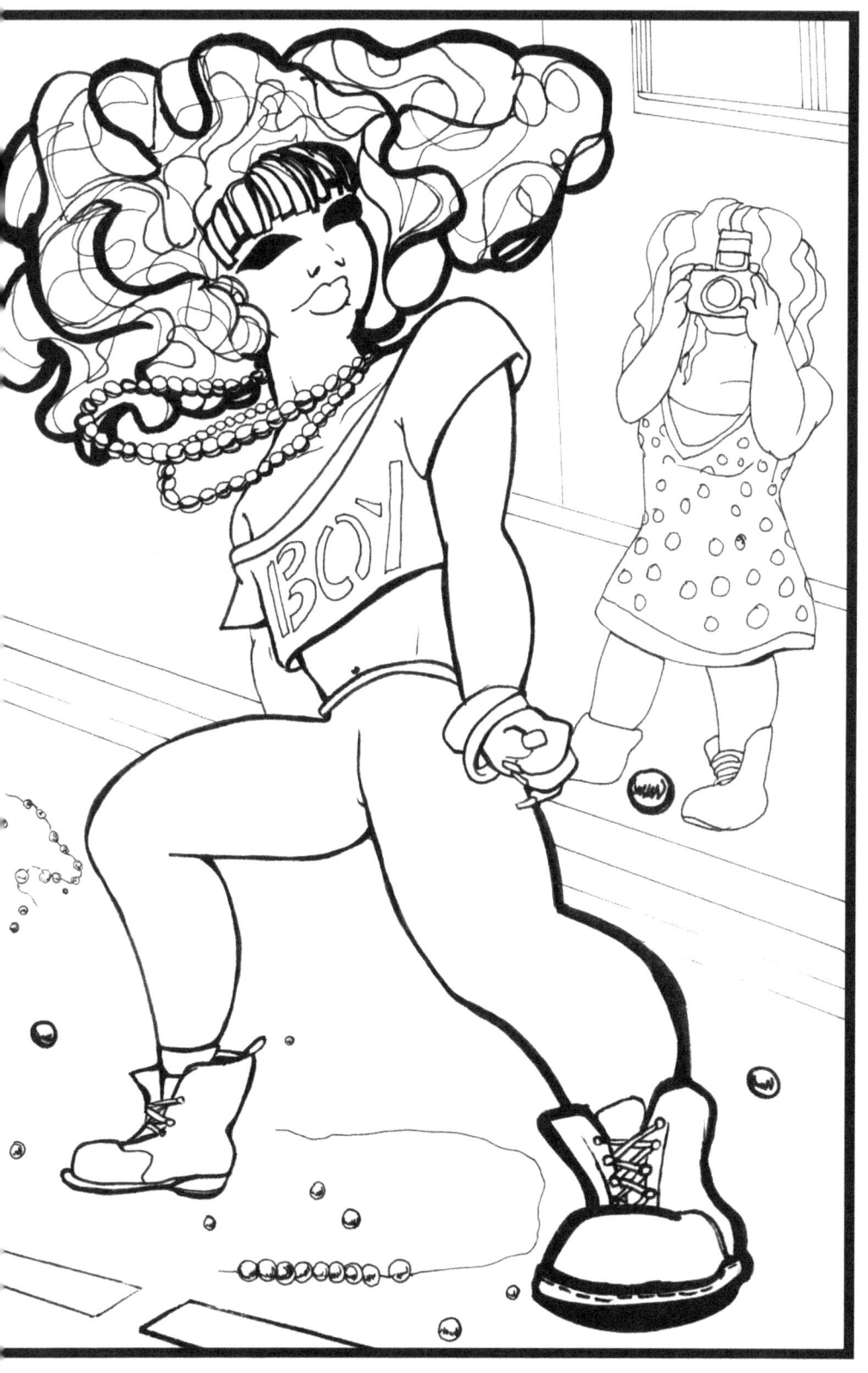

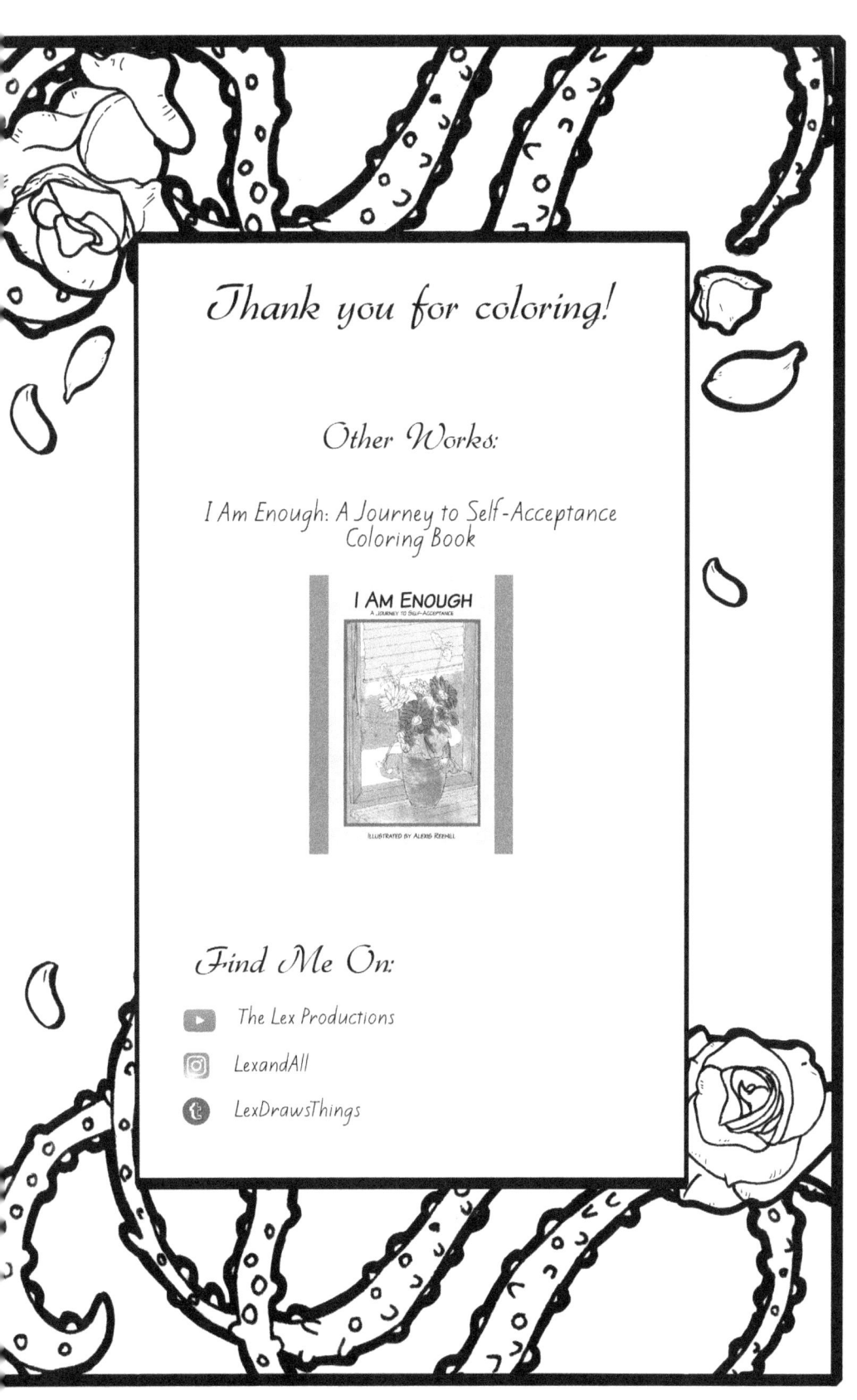

Thank you for coloring!

Other Works:

I Am Enough: A Journey to Self-Acceptance Coloring Book

Find Me On:

- The Lex Productions
- LexandAll
- LexDrawsThings

www.ingramcontent.com/pod-product-compliance
Lightning Source LLC
Chambersburg PA
CBHW070250230526
45470CB00002B/558